CW01020592

Professional

Sound Reinforcement TECHNIQUES

Tips and Tricks of a Concert Sound Engineer

by Jim Yakabuski

MIX BOOKS®

236 Georgia Street, Suite 100
Vallejo, CA 94590

©2001 artistpro.com, LLC
All Rights Reserved. No portion of the book may be reproduced, copied, transmitted, or stored in any mechanical or electronic form without the written permission of the publisher.

Library of Congress Catalog Card Number: 2001087510

Production Staff: Mike Lawson, Publisher; Patrick Runkle, Editorial Director;
Stephen Ramirez, Art Director; Jessica Westcott, Editorial Assistant.
All Photos © 1994 Michael Carroll. All rights reserved.

MixBooks is an imprint of artistpro.com, LLC
236 Georgia Street, Suite 100
Vallejo, CA 94590
707-554-1935

Also from MixBooks
The AudioPro Home Recording Course, Volumes I, II, and III
I Hate the Man Who Runs This Bar!
How to Make Money Scoring Soundtracks and Jingles
The Art of Mixing: A Visual Guide to Recording, Engineering, and Production
The Mixing Engineer's Handbook
The Mastering Engineer's Handbook
Music Publishing: The Real Road to Music Business Success, Rev. and Exp. 4th Ed.
How to Run a Recording Session
The Professional Musician's Internet Guide
The Songwriters Guide to Collaboration, Rev. and Exp. 2nd Ed.
Critical Listening and Auditory Perception
Modular Digital Multitracks: The Power User's Guide, Rev. Ed.
The Dictionary of Music Business Terms
Professional Microphone Techniques
Sound for Picture, 2nd Ed.
Music Producers, 2nd Ed.
Live Sound Reinforcement

Also from EMBooks
The Independent Working Musician
Making the Ultimate Demo, 2nd Ed.
Remix: The Electronic Music Explosion
Making Music with Your Computer, 2nd Ed.
Anatomy of a Home Studio
The EM Guide to the Roland VS-880

Printed in Auburn Hills, MI
ISBN 1-931140-06-5

Dedication

This book is dedicated to Jamie and my girls.
You give my life inspiration and make coming home the best part of it all.

Acknowledgements

I'd like to thank all of the talented sound engineers who contributed to my education and training throughout my entire career. For the many unsung sound mixers who trudged across the frozen tundra of the western Canadian bar circuit and took the time to "have a listen" to my PA and offer suggestions, thanks! It was your guidance and instruction that gave me the hope and confidence to pursue a career when my chops were so bad. To Harry Witz of dB Sound, the first American to give me a chance to tour and learn the world of concert sound, I offer special thanks, you were the break I needed and I've never forgotten that. To all the bands who have allowed me the honor of mixing them throughout the years: Ted Nugent, Julio Iglesias, Engelbert Humperdinck, Luis Miguel, Extreme, Aerosmith, Poison, Gin Blossoms, Jon Secada, and especially Van Halen, who gave a monitor mixer the chance to become a front-of-house mixer and cut my teeth with the greatest rock and roll band of our time. Al, Ed, Mike and Sammy (and Gary), you guys are the best. Special thanks to Scotty Ross for believing in me and opening that door.

I'd also like to thank all the fine audio techs who have been a part of the tours we've done together. Fumi, thanks for coming back for more again and again. I'd especially like to thank Jerry Harvey and Dave Lawler who forced me into a new way of thinking about audio, one that stretched my boundaries and made me better.

Many thanks to Mike Lawson of artistpro.com for giving me the chance to get these "notes from the road" passed on to the next generation of tour bus dwellers. Special thanks to Patrick Runkle and Jessica Westcott for editorial guidance and to Stephen Ramirez for transforming my daily tour journels into the book you now hold in your hand.

Finally I'd like to thank Mario Educate and the entire staff at OSA who are in the process of educating me all over again.

Foreword

There have been many manuals written on the "how to" of professional sound reinforcement techniques. Most of the information is gathered through academic study or by practical experience, as the live audio field develops.

One of the most exciting things I find about this profession is that the live sound industry is barely three decades old. In my mind, the first "large scale" concert audio system was assembled for Woodstock in 1969. That system of barely 10,000 passive watts for 500,000 people planted, with audio chronics, the seeds of curiosity to innovate hardware and practices that make up our daily regimen today. There are few careers one can choose (outside of the dot-com and computer industries) that are still in the early developmental stages.

As we enter the next century, the days of simple audio systems requiring only basic knowledge are gone forever. These days, the consummate audio person is expected to have a myriad of well-honed technical and artistic skills. We have also seen the front-of-house mixing engineer's original job description be divided, with the system engineer—who often is not only a specialist in design and implementation of the speaker system, but also in measurement and EQ—forming a combined team with the mix engineer.

This team not only conquers technical challenges, but also has a responsibility to be part of the "funnel of cultural transfer" between the artist and the audience. With ticket prices and expectations being what they are today, every seat in the house deserves high-quality audio.

Before concerts, I am often asked how someone can "get started" in live sound, or people want me to "name a school" in the live sound business. There are several colleges that offer courses, but I am always at a partial loss to recommend a book, or manual, which offers both practical explanations as well as insider "tips" that many audio pros are reluctant to share with their colleagues or students. I am pleased that such a book now exists, and you're holding it in your hands.

I have had the pleasure of working on several musical tours with "Jim Yak." We endeavored to raise the bar of what a front-of-house mix and system engineer could accomplish, and teamwork was the word *du jour.*

In the following chapters, Jim has compiled the highlights of his experience in the live audio field over the last eighteen years. Beginners and seasoned engineers alike will find the tips and pointers educational and thought provoking. I invite you to enjoy it.

Dave Lawler
DOCKTRDAVE AUDIO INC.

Introduction

It all started in the summer of 1981. After carefully considering my career options, I decided to pursue my love for sound and music by enrolling in a studio engineering class at a recording studio in Vancouver, Canada. The course lasted six weeks and, although the acquired knowledge was sure to pay dividends down the road, I felt slightly confined in the studio environment. I happily accepted a chance to mix my friend's rock and roll band as they began their touring career.

Armed with just enough information to be truly dangerous, we equipped ourselves with a rather expensive PA system—purchased collectively by four of the six members of the band and the barely legal assistance of our drummer, who moonlighted as a senior loans officer at a bank—and loaded in to our first gig. I clearly remember standing behind the console that first night realizing I had barely more than a clue as to what I was doing.

The first set barreled along, and just as I began to feel comfortable in the saddle, an ominous long howl arose from the depths, encompassing the room. I looked around in panic and reached for the master fader, bringing it down just enough to stop the whirling demon from taking over our entire beings. Just as the perspiration began to dry from my brow and my pulse rate dropped to a reasonable level, the moaning death chant of 100 Hz feedback returned to search for more tortured souls.

The band walked off stage several minutes later to find me shaking my perplexed head in disbelief at the turn of events. How could this be happening to me? I had never heard such rumblings in the cozy studio where our classes were held. Luckily for me, the band was not schooled in issues such as these, and had no answers themselves. We were left to ponder this problem.

Suddenly, from the smoky depths of the bar two dark figures came into focus. The long hair and tattered jeans told me these weren't loan officers or grocery clerks such as I. These were musicians. The genuine article. Our knights in shining armor. They swaggered up to the mix area and kindly introduced themselves. "It seems like you're having a bit of feedback trouble." "Ya, I guess so," I replied. "I'm not sure what's going on." "I noticed you don't have an equalizer in your sound system," spoke one of the wise and grungy longhairs. "We're rehearsing just up the block. We'd be glad to lend you one to get through the night."

I knew I had reached a defining moment in my life. I was quite certain the next words to exit my mouth would make or break my career and pave the way to success or failure. I carefully considered their generous offer while glancing at the faces of my bandmates, sensing their trust and confidence in me was riding on my response and professionalism. I turned to the good Samaritans. "Thanks," I replied, "but I don't see how that will help." From these humble beginnings came the spark that set the flame burning to pass on the knowledge I have gathered throughout my years of mixing live music.

This book has been an ongoing venture that began in 1993 on the Van Halen World Tour. As I went about my daily routine of setting up, tuning, soundchecking and mixing the show, I realized that there were certain habits and recurring processes that I followed every day to make things sound the best that they could sound. It was then that I remembered my first few years on the road and the struggles I went through trying to go from rookie student to tenured sound engineer. I read all the audio magazines I could get my hands on but found few books that related to the day-to-day process of what we did in the clubs of western Canada. Many audio books covered the theory of audio, described sound in terms of wavelengths and formulae, and gave useful details on how to construct an impedance-matching transformer. But they all seemed to fail at describing the essential skills of being a mixing engineer.

Don't get me wrong: I highly recommend that we all get as much education on the basics of audio and the theory behind its operation. Once the groundwork has been laid, however, the next step is to train our ears, and learn to operate the equipment in an organized and effective manner. If you have any aspirations at all to mix shows, then you have found a book that will help you to use the tools of the trade, and develop insights to be more effective in your thought processes and techniques.

A short time before starting this book, a title hit the shelves of bookstores and pro shops called *Harvey Pennick's Little Red Book.* It's a collection of quick tips and bits of wisdom from the legendary golf instructor. Golf is a passion of mine, and I was amazed at the simplicity of the concepts in the book and the matter-of-fact, no-nonsense instruction.

The quick tips that make up my book are observations of daily practices that have become habit for me and make my day flow more smoothly. They were jotted down haphazardly as I went about my day, relating to the process I was involved in at the time. The tips are organized into chapters which follow the course of a sound engineer's day, from load-in to load-out, but the knowledge passed on doesn't always follow a theoretical theme, it simply provides point-of attack information to solve real-life audio issues. I must say now that these are not audio theories or rock solid techniques that will work for everyone; they are descriptions of techniques that work for me. I hope they work for you.

Lastly, I have sprinkled some humor within the pages of these bits of wisdom. I believe we are doing a very serious job, but I also insist that I have fun as I do it. I hope you will appreciate the light-hearted feel of this book and enjoy reading it as much as I enjoyed writing it. Try to keep open minded and flexible. Your approach and style will change many times as you move forward. If you allow yourself to learn, you will find much wisdom out there that can be used to your advantage. A great mix is well appreciated by every listener, and the payoff for you is the satisfaction of knowing you have made people very happy.

Good luck and God bless.
Jim Yakabuski

Contents

PART SIX: SHOWTIME

PART ONE: PRE-PRODUCTION

PRE-PRODUCTION

This is where it all begins. The success of your tour will often be determined here, in the planning stages. This is the time to design your PA, and get your design approved by the budget makers.

The decisions you make now concerning console layout, signal path, and speaker zones will stay with you for the length of the tour. If you take the time to consider the style of music, average size of venue, and volume requirements in these early stages, you will have a much better chance of getting "it" right night after night.

Before you get to the first "real" page of the book, I want to let you know how it was created. Often-repeated audio practices and techniques that were a part of my day-to-day routine went into a notebook that has lived in my back pocket for the past seven years. These notes to myself represent a collage of the wide spectrum of skills that make up mixing a great live show.

To make some sense of all these useful—but sometimes unrelated—notes, we tried to place them into chapters and subchapters. Most of these memos cover more than one topic, and have the potential to live in several other chapters in the book.

I placed these notes in "pre-production," however, because I think they speak loudly to the importance of making design choices before the fact. The importance is not only in choosing gear, but also in organizing notes and documents that will affect the way you mix the show, as well as in handling rehearsal time in an efficient manner and dealing with the production team and musicians in the most effective way.

For those of you who define pre-production as a single phone call to a sound provider for a one-off show and a two-hour rehearsal with the band, there is info here for you as well. We don't all get a month on a sound stage to work with the system and song list, but we can all be prepared going into whatever size show we are mixing. Make accurate equipment advance lists, lay your console out in an efficient way, and know in advance who's playing guitar in the intro to song one of the set list.

You haven't done a show yet. But it's coming soon. There will be days when the endless musical rehearsals have you wishing you had pursued a career in dental hygiene, but hang in there. It won't be long until the house lights fade, the fans start cheering, and the first downbeat of the first show of a yearlong tour kicks off.

That is when you'll know without a doubt why you're a professional live sound engineer.

CHAPTER 1

Building Your PA

Get out a paper and pencil. How many channels will you need to mic up the whole band? Will you need a second console? How about effects? Should you use one reverb for the lead singer or reverb and delay?

These are the things to ask yourself long before load-in. As soon as you know you have the gig and you have an idea of what gear you'll be using, start defining the nuts and bolts of your system. How many speakers do you need? Or better yet, how many can you have? You're building your PA. It's a great time, both creative and exhilarating. Make the most of it. Be an architect!

"MAP OUT YOUR DRIVE"

7/14/97 Ted Nugent

It's great to do a one-off gig and have everyone in the sound department—both your crew and the local guys—on the same page. It should start weeks before the gig when you advance it. If you're given a budget that allows for anything more than "take what you get," speaking with the sound provider and plotting a patch plan for the system weeks in advance will minimize confusion come gig day.

It is important to discuss the console type and speakers he or she can provide, how many gates and compressors you'll need, and many other system details, but it is equally imperative to discuss how the PA will be stacked, flown, and wired. You can't always know ahead of time what the venue requires with regards to speaker coverage, but often the sound company representative can give you a pretty good idea of the size and geometry of the building.

From this information, you can map out a patch schematic of their drive system. By this I mean you can decide ahead of time how many speakers will be used for a particular zone ("long throw" for example), including which crossover and EQ will be used to control that group of speakers. If this is discussed early in the planning stages, the sound company has a chance to let you know how many speakers can be used for each zone to match up with their power amp configurations. They can also let you know how many EQs and crossovers they can give you.

When you arrive at the gig, make sure someone from the sound company is present who is aware of your prior advance work, and then hand a drawing of the wiring scheme to all the sound guys who will be patching the system. If everyone working with the PA that day knows which amplifiers are driving which speakers, and the corresponding zone they are in, component checks and troubleshooting will go so much smoother.

Also, if you are using a multiple-zone system that day, you will have many crossovers to set and program. Even though you have planned all of this, it's a great idea to have a map of the routing to help you keep things organized. The goal of the day is zero confusion. If everyone is on the same page and that page is a map, you have a better chance of getting to your destination on time.

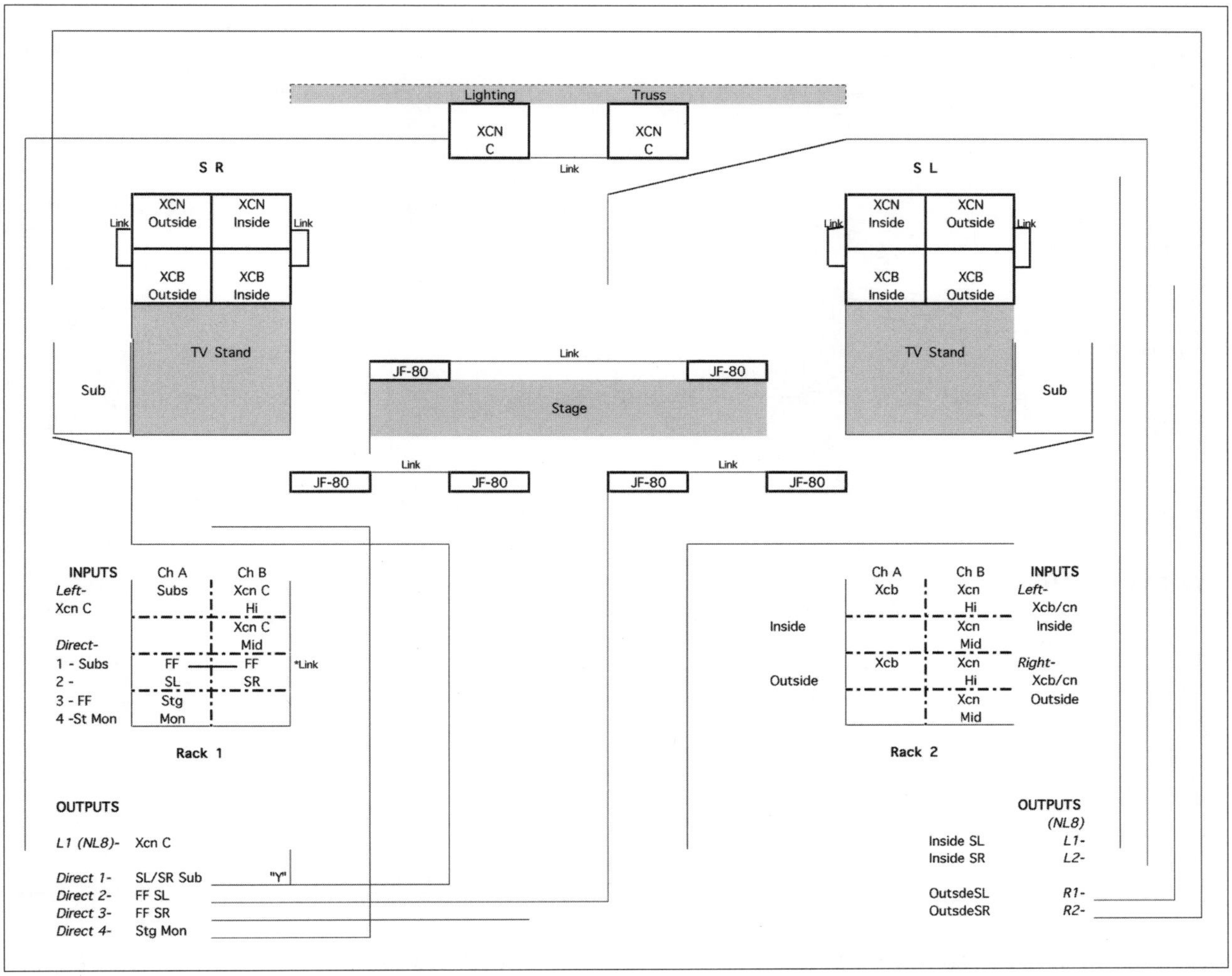

This is an example of a simple diagram, done in Microsoft Excel. Although some squinting might be necessary, you can follow speaker cable output routing to the various speakers and trace input patching to each corresponding amp channel. If you walk in the room with this, you stand a much better chance of patching the amp rack and speakers correctly the first time.

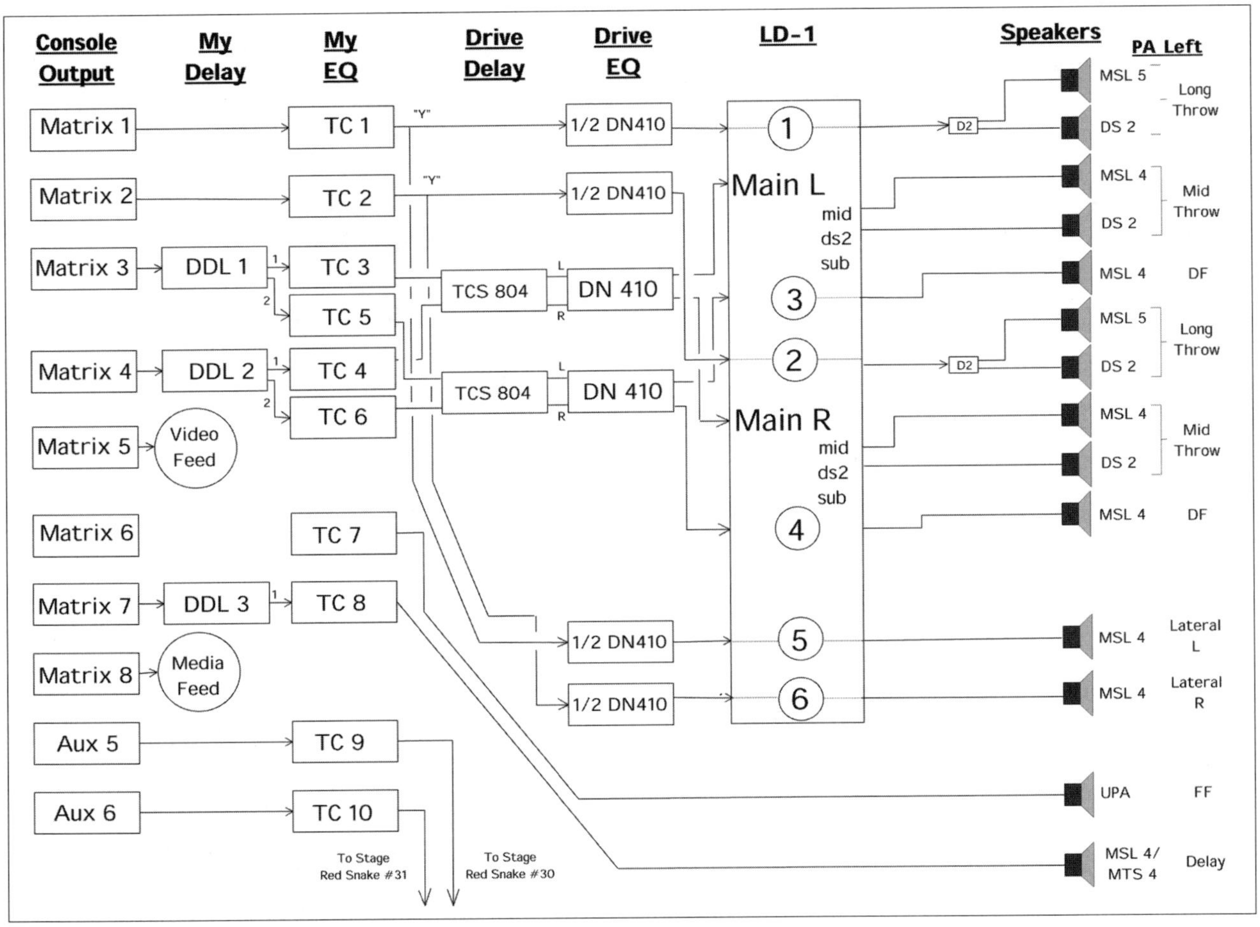

This diagram follows signal flow from the console Matrix outputs to my touring package delay and EQ, and then on to the rented drive system's delay, EQ, Crossover/Processor and then to the speakers. The rental system consisted of a drive system (delay, EQ, and speakers) that we carried through Spain to save on shipping all our gear overseas.

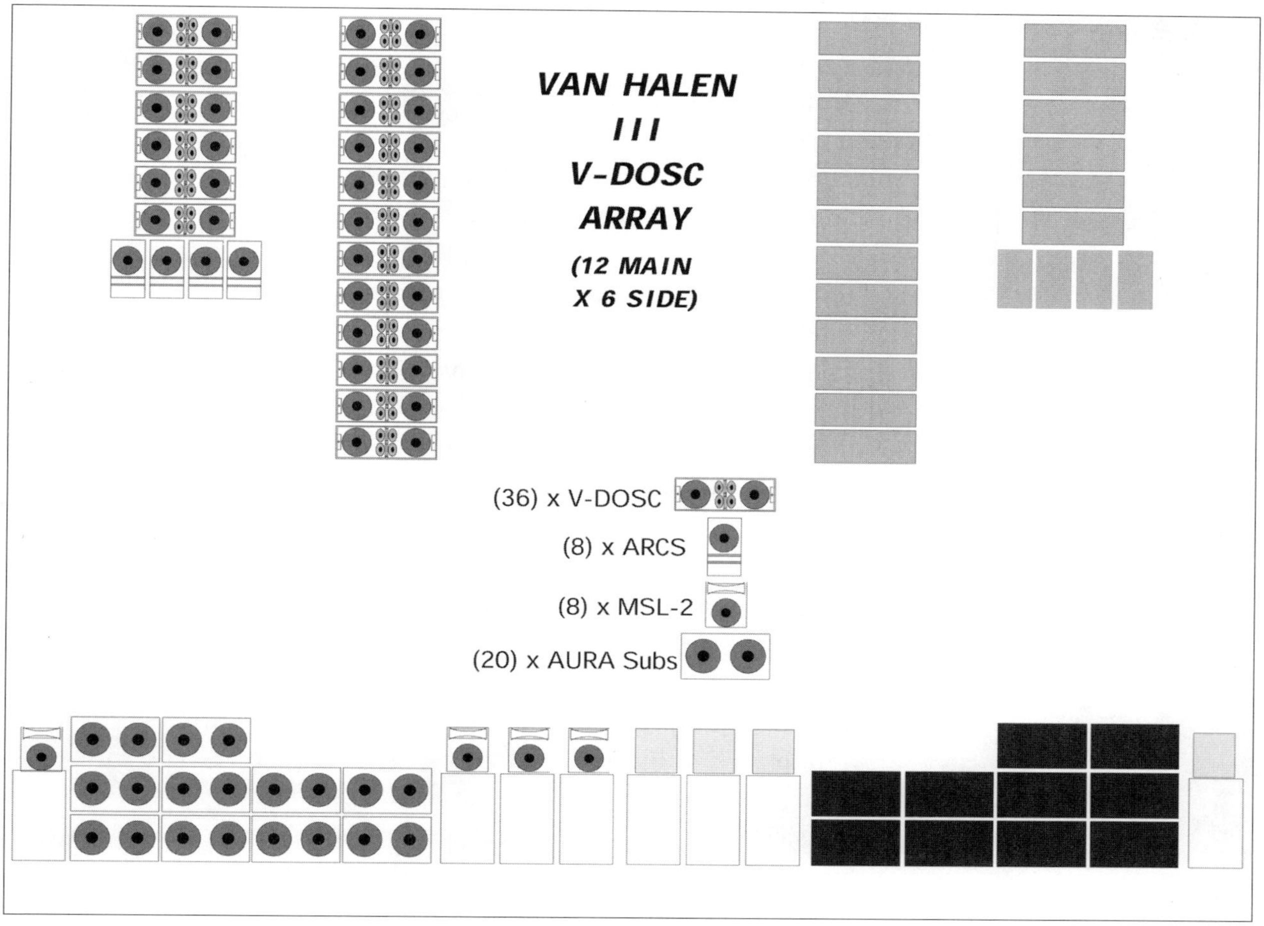

This is a CAD drawing of our 1998 Van Halen touring system. By drawing a version of your speaker without the grill cloth on, you can be specific about details such as "horn up" or "horn down." This type of drawing is great for those situations where you are using a local audio provider and you just want to get the ball rolling in the direction of how to divide the PA speakers into clusters.

4/10/96 Julio Iglesias

Old sound engineers never die, they just move to Vegas and run sound for singers our parents listened to.

Well, at least that happened to some sound engineers that I know, including myself for a short time. It was a bit of a learning curve moving from mixing mostly rock and pop bands to artists that were without a doubt the only star of the show. Their names are on the marquee, and the fans buying the tickets want to be sure to hear that singer's golden pipes well above any musical distraction.

What I discovered early in my new career direction was that conventional mixing didn't necessarily work, and I would continually chase my tail. First, I'd turn up a keyboard patch, and then I'd turn down the percussion. Soon I'd reach for a guitar mic, and then ... Well, you get the picture. The funny thing was, as I would reach up to turn something down, the musicians were already backing off the gas pedal, having spent years mixing themselves on stage. What I learned was, never let the star vocalist get lost in the mix as you play the game of "chase the offending instrument."

The simplest way to make sure I'm not losing the vocalist is to group everything except the star vocal into one VCA group. This way I can mix the show with two fingers. One is on the band and one on the star. If some part of the band gets too loud, I turn the whole band mix down to ensure the vocalist is clear and on top and then sort out the culprit before fading the whole band mix back in.

This all may sound a bit extreme, but you can't really know how tough these gigs can be until you try them. It doesn't often happen that a fan will come out of the audience at the end of the show and mention to you that the keyboards were a touch low. You *know* you will hear, and usually your boss will as well, if his vocals were not the primary element of the mix. Make your life easy and group everything except the star on one VCA.

The musicians in the band are usually not around more than a couple years at a time, and we sound engineers come and go from those gigs as well, but that star will be in Vegas well into the twenty-first century, so do your duty and let the fans hear him or her as clear as crystal.

"GROUP RATES"

2/17/98 Van Halen

OK. Let's face it. It's all about money, right? In this day and age of cutting back on costs, we have all been forced to cut corners and rethink how we approach the necessity of certain equipment. We've also been asked to minimize our footprint on the front-of-house riser. One way that space can be saved is by cutting back on the amount of compressors you take on the road.

On a recent tour, I put the main instruments and most of the vocals that needed to be compressed into stereo subgroups and then inserted stereo compressors across those groups. One rack space, one stereo compressor, and a whole group of vocals or instruments are processed. End result: a lot of space was saved.

With the new consoles on the scene now, loaded with virtual dynamics and onboard software-driven signal processing, the days of racks and racks of gates, compressors, and effects units are soon to be gone. We are also seeing "8-in, 8-out" interface devices, such as BSS Soundweb, that process the signal in a bunch of ways; this further eliminates rack-mounted compressors and EQ units.

I agree with this philosophy of downsizing when it comes to tours that go for a long period of time, where things get set and pretty much left alone. When I do a one-off and have very little time to get set up, however, sitting down with a mouse and new software is a scary thought, and definitely not the fastest way to go.

That being said, the onboard stuff is really close (at the time of this writing) to being just as great sounding, and user-friendly to operate, as the rack-mounted stuff. We are already seeing rack mounted consoles that operate with a mouse and screen, or small mainframes with a few VCA's and channel strips to replace the monoliths we now mix on. The learning curve may be a bit steep, but when the first big tour goes out there with a front-of-house riser that is 8' x 8', we are all going to have to follow suit. Because I've seen this coming, I have tried to consolidate my rack space and get used to the "downsizing mindset."

One great way to accomplish this is to gang those compressors up into subgroups. It works well. You may lose a little control over individual vocals or instruments, but on average you will be just as pleased and keep costs and real estate requirements down. Let's get with the new way of thinking and keep ourselves employed. And if you're still not convinced, think of all the P-touch labels that you'll save not having to mark all those compressors at the start of the tour.

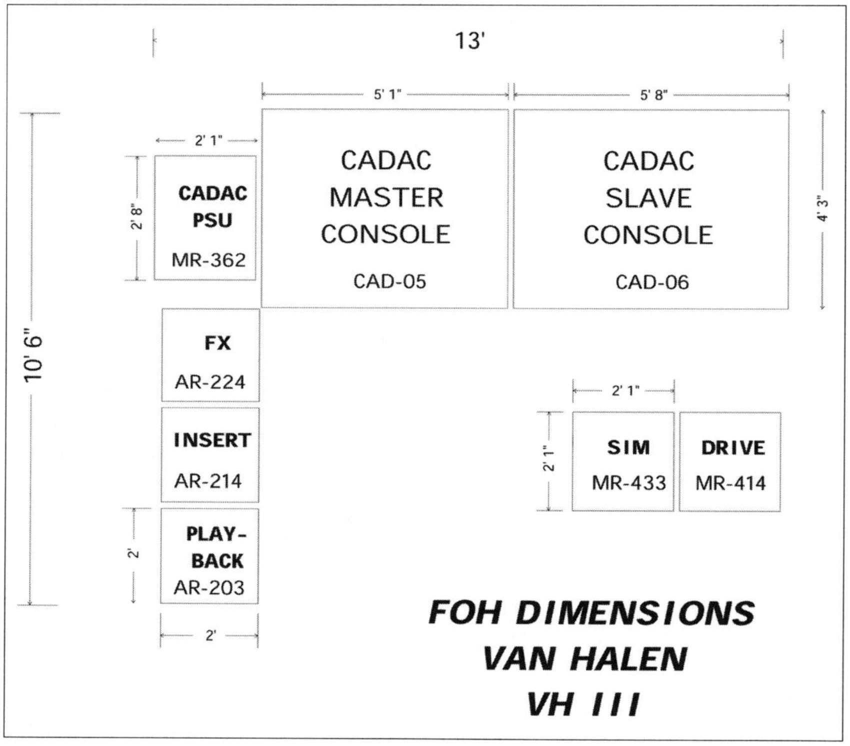

Measuring your front-of-house setup and then drawing a diagram is very helpful to your Production Manager, your records, and your day-to-day setup when space might be tight. To avoid struggling every day to make it all fit, consolidate processing gear whenever you can.

"AND YOU THOUGHT YOU'D NEVER USE DIVISION AFTER HIGH SCHOOL"

10/15/96 Julio Iglesias

Well, you were wrong. Today, we are going to learn how to divide up our PA systems. We're going to put them into neat little sections so we can control level, EQ, and time alignment separately. OK, pick up your pencils and put on your thinking caps because this is Audio 101, and you're going to learn how to be a sound engineer.

Ok, Ok. Here's the real lesson: The best way to successfully cover the entire room or listening area is to have separate control over all quadrants of the PA, whether they are facing in different directions or overlapping each other. As you grow more successful as a sound engineer and mix in bigger and bigger venues, you will undoubtedly discover that a pile of boxes pointing straight ahead can sound great at the front-of-house board, but the same boxes, aimed off to the side, can wound the clientele with volume and incorrect EQ if not dealt with properly.

The solution is to divide your PA into different zones and control them with as many variables (level, EQ, delay, and crossover) as your budget will allow. If said budget is strict enough to limit your control to putting these side speakers on a separate amp channel only, at least affording you to turn their volume down, then take what you can get. If you can put an EQ on that section, or run those speakers off a different matrix on your console, by all means go for it.

Being able to control different zones from the console makes so much sense, although the controlling factor is usually how many crossovers you have. Each zone you designate has to be processed separately to allow true control, and this is where the money starts to pile up. The other problem is that it just gets too complicated and time consuming for some people. Sometimes the entire PA can sound great with the same EQ and a few amp level adjustments. Don't get bogged down with EQ'ing ten zones only to find that when you turn them all on together they sound awful. Be careful with delaying zones separately as this can cause more grief than good if your settings are wrong.

If your best friend is a SIM operator, buy him lunch as often as you can to use his knowledge of EQ'ing and delaying multiple zones. If you don't even know what SIM is, don't feel bad. It's a computer program that does analyzes sound; it's also an art form and science that some people believe in and some don't, so if you don't know what you're missing, don't fret.

Using some kind of measurement system to accurately delay each speaker zone is all you should be concerned with. There is a lot to be said for control, and if you can achieve control over the various zones of your sound system, you are ahead of the game.

Some examples of how you might divide up the PA to control separately are: long throw, lateral or side fill (around the sides of the room), down fill (if you're flying the PA this sometimes works better than front fill because the speakers are not blocked when people stand up front), and front fill. Delay speakers are beneficial if the venue is very long and your main speakers just aren't making it all the way to the back. If you're doing a bunch of one-offs with a band, and you're using a local sound company everywhere you go, try to gather info on the style and shape of the venue and advance a PA that fits into your budget, yet covers the room adequately with as much control as possible.

Make your grade school teachers proud and master the art of division!

"IN YOUR FACE, MAN!"

9/08/95 Van Halen

Have you ever had one of those shows where it seemed you were reaching for the headphones every ten seconds, trying to distinguish one thing from another, as it just wasn't clear in the PA yet? A handy bit of equipment that takes some of this hassle away is a set of near-field monitors set up on the top of your console to act as a second way to solo things up.

I'll start by saying that for many sound engineers and PA owners, this is a bit of an extravagance, so don't think this is one of those things that you can't live without. But you can make this as simple as a cheap pair of speakers, powered with whatever is left lying around (a spare power amp or single rack-space headphone amp), with the signal to the amp sent from the control room or PFL output, if your console has these.

Some guys like to line check in the afternoon with their monitors. I'm a recent convert to this, but I warn that if there's ambient noise around when you're line checking, you may not hear buzzes or tonal peculiarities as well as you can with headphones. During the show, you can quickly solo up what you want to listen to in the monitors and avoid reaching for the headphones.

Another great use for near-field monitors is in situations where you're having trouble hearing the PA because you're stuck in a bad mix location, or bad weather has forced you to cover up outdoors and your ability to hear the sound system is hampered. In this kind of situation it's good to blend in your near-field monitors to give back some edge. The trick to making this work is delaying the send to your monitors, so that the monitor sound reaches your ears at the same time as the PA. For this you will need to send the signal from the control room "out" on your mixer to a delay, and from there to your power source which connects to your monitor speakers. (See Chapter 10, "Delay Measurements," to read up on setting correct delay.)

The way to set up your near-field speakers to work as sweeteners in conjunction with the PA is to first listen to the PA in the main part of the room. When this reference is fresh in your mind, go back to the console where things are a little dull or shaded from the speakers and slowly bring in the monitors until they give you a more accurate top-end picture.

Compare your listening position at the console (with your monitor speakers included) with what most of the audience is hearing. You can then reference correctly at show time.

This isn't for everyone, and some people prefer to use only headphones, but if the opportunity presents itself, give this a try and see if it helps you out.

"DISCOVER THE BENEFITS OF SHOCK THERAPY"

4/19/95 Van Halen

Everything has become fairly neat and tidy these days. In the good old days there was a certain "big rock" look to having a pile of mic stands around the drum kit with mics pointing in from all directions. A while back drummers started mounting all of the toms on drum racks; soon after, the cymbals were mounted from this rack as well.

The natural progression from there was to have the sound guys get rid of the messy drum mic stands and mount the mics from the drum hardware on the rack. When this is done effectively, it can really clean up the look of a drum kit and it is quite convenient and speedy for us sound guys.

One problem that arises from this setup, though, is that the thump and bump of toms being hit and the shock that is transferred down the cymbal stands to the drum rack (and through anything that is attached) can lead to low-end rumble in your drum mics. I have had situations where putting the high-pass filter in on the mic itself as well as using all of the high-pass capabilities on the mixing board channel still didn't filter out the rumble.

The first thing to do in an effort to solve this problem is to isolate the source of the rumble. I have found that it usually appears in a cymbal mic or overhead. These condenser mics are quite sensitive to low-end handling noise. If there is just one mic that is receiving the shock rumble, you may discover that something is resting on the mic stand or some kind of physical connection is causing the problem. The best thing I've found to cure this problem has been the use of some foam insulation tape which can be rapped around the base of the mic stand boom where it is attached to the drum rack. Some kind of insulation between the two pieces of metal will most likely cure or reduce the effect.

Of course, with cymbal mics, you can try setting the mics in shock isolation mounts that can usually be purchased from the mic manufacturer. These mic attachments often have the mic floating in some type of rubber band configuration, which detaches it from any kind of physical connection with the mic stand.

In one situation we had a big problem because we had tried everything and there seemed to be no clear solution. The ride cymbal, when struck, would send a resonance through the tom mics and the only solution seemed to be heavy tom mic gating, which this drummer would not allow. Eventually the drum tech changed the ride cymbal to a slightly lighter-gauge model and the problem was alleviated. Because of this, I realized that the cymbal stands should also be shock mounted with the insulation tape to minimize rumble.

Preparing your drum rack from the beginning, when you have the time, will get you ahead of the game so that the problems won't creep up when you don't have time to fix them.

"WE SHALL HEAR NO BACKGROUND VOCAL BEFORE ITS TIME"

1/15/95 Van Halen

It's amazing how much leakage can come from the background vocal mics on stage when the singer steps away from that mic. When they are not singing, there is no reason to have that mic on, and when they are singing, the singer's head is between the mic and whatever else is roaring on stage so the bleed is cut down considerably.

The answer is clear; the mic should only be turned on when the background vocalist is singing. This is easier said than done. I'm sure every one of us who has tried muting and unmuting the mics has been caught opening the mics up a little too late or missing a cue altogether. This can go unnoticed if you are a front-of-house mixer, but if you are the monitor mixer you can find yourself in the "Chateau Bow Wow" over this.

So the quest was on to try to find a way to automatically shut off vocal mics when the singers step away from them. I'm sure we've all tried using a very loose and sensitive noise gate, and this can work, but can also cause you mucho embarrassment if the singer starts to cut in and out when speaking or singing quietly.

Another method that worked quite well was the trigger mat. I used this on a couple of tours. The theory was that a thin rubber mat was placed where the background singer would stand and upon standing on the mat a tone was triggered that would open the noise gate (via the key trigger input) and subsequently open the microphone. This worked great until it *didn't* work, which happened occasionally.

The best solution I've found to date is a little infrared trigger device made by a company called D3 that is placed between the mic cable and the mic. It sends out a little infrared beam of light, and when someone steps into the beam of light, it opens the microphone gate circuit. It operates along the same principle as the automatic toilet flushers in most public restrooms. When you step into the light, it triggers the toilet to flush after you step out of the light. These little D3 gates are really tiny and easy to manage. They have been improved to deal with phantom-powered condenser mics, and now they even run without batteries if you engage the +48V phantom power on the console channel. The cleanup of unwanted noise on stage and in the front-of-house mix is incredible and you will never miss another cue.

Try these devices when you get a chance or create a successful gating system that works for you. You will really notice a difference in unwanted bleed from mics that you don't need to be on until someone is singing.

"STICK IT TO THEM"

7/11/94 Ted Nugent

The longer we tour, the more complex and technical the gear gets. It used to be enough to have a mono, two-way PA, and if you were really cool, you had a tape echo and an EQ to jazz things up.

Well, times have changed. If you're just getting started in this business and you've walked by the front-of-house or monitor positions at your local arena before a big concert, you were probably overwhelmed with the amount of "stuff" those guys managed to stick into the racks. I know that when I started we had a very basic PA, and I would go to a show and try to imagine how someone might possibly use all that gear and keep track of how the signal was going in and out of it.

The secret for me has always been clear and concise labeling. I have worked with people who don't have a single label on any of 15 compressors in their racks, and I can't for the life of me figure out how they know what they're adjusting in the dark during a show. I don't have the time to count down from the top piece of gear, or the guts to risk adjusting the wrong knob while the show is going on. So, during the prep time for a tour, I'll take the trusty Brother P-touch, or similar labeling device (good old white electrical tape has done the job for years), and label away. I've even been cool beyond my own belief and color coded my labeling so that an EQ, crossover, delay and group out on the console all have the same color tape to keep signal flow clear in my mind. (I know; I scare myself sometimes, and you can hold the anal-retentive jokes.)

I will often group things in racks in a sensible way to keep the order of signal flow a little easier to follow. Keeping it clear is especially helpful when you are doing a one-off with a local sound company. You know what I mean: You call ahead and order a bunch of stuff for your front-of-house racks. Come gig day, all this gear shows up in racks arranged in ways you wouldn't dream of arranging it.

The first thing I do in this situation is pull out the pack of sticky labels and decide which compressor is for what, and even label reverb units and effects so that I know which unit I'm changing programs on during the show. If you do this even before you begin patching all your signal processing to your console, you will stand a much better chance of getting it right the first time. This will help more than you can ever imagine when the show is in full swing and you reach down to adjust that bass guitar compressor. If it is clearly labeled, you will never second-guess a fast move of the knob; you can just do your adjusting at the compressor and get back to the business of mixing.

The same goes for console labeling. Label those matrix and aux outputs every time, just like you mark down which channel is which mic. I hate it when I have to think about which aux is the vocal verb and which one is the drum verb. Make it clear and, as they say in New York, "forget about it."

"THE ROYAL TREATMENT"

4/22/96 Julio Iglesias

It always seems to come back to this: We originally built these things we call PA systems so that the 'public' could be 'addressed' in such a way as to hear what a person had to say or sing, but music and crowd noise made it awfully hard for a singer to be heard on his or her own lungpower. So we built these black boxes and handed the singer a microphone. But pretty soon we turned up the drums so loud that the guitar couldn't be heard, and so we turned up the guitar a bunch and then we couldn't hear the vocals, and so on. I think you get the picture.

PAs were originally designed to allow us to hear the singer's sweet pipes above the din. For this reason, I always strive to maintain clarity and level on a singer's voice. One tool that aids in this endeavor is, of course, an equalizer.

Usually, the process of EQ'ing the whole sound system is misdirected when we make slight adjustments to the main system EQ to accommodate the sound of the vocal. With that vocal out there on top of the mix, it is inevitable that the system EQ (the main Left/Right EQ) will start to receive cuts and bumps for the sole purpose of making the main vocal mic sound better.

One approach that I began doing a while back was designating a separate EQ strictly for the lead vocal. The usual method is to insert it in the channel or subgroup, or put it in line with the compressor or whatever you have inserted on that vocal. The type of EQ is simply a matter of choice. Some people prefer a five- or six-band parametric and some like a good old 31-band graphic EQ. The advantage to this is that by cutting out and shaping the lead vocal on an EQ separate from the mains, you leave the main system EQ "flat" for the rest of the band instruments to sound full. This follows the premise that the lead vocal generally sits on top of the mix, and the feedback that will potentially occur, as well as the tonal shaping of the sound system, generally comes from one microphone.

You usually wind up with a vocal EQ that resembles what the system EQ would have looked like, and you are free to have a more solid starting point from which to touch up the EQ on the rest of the instruments. By treating that lead vocal mic with a little extra care and attention you will always reap the benefits of your labor, and the lead singer will probably buy you a dinner or two.

"ADDING A RHYTHM GUITARIST WITHOUT PAYING A SALARY"

7/10/93 Van Halen

The good old days of the heavy metal power trio are almost gone. It seems the majority of the new bands today have a couple of guitar players and maybe some keyboards. One problem with mixing a power trio always seemed to be the emptiness in the rhythm chunk when the lone guitarist would go for a solo. With only the bass guitarist left to fill in all that space in the chunk of the mix, things can sound thin during the guitar solos. Having mixed quite a few of these power trio bands, I searched for a way to fill things in.

When you are mixing a band that has the guitar and the guitarist featured, it is really important to make sure his or her rhythm sound is distinct and not obscured. Because of this priority, I've found I will usually center the bass guitar EQ primarily in the lower frequencies to leave lots of space in the mix for the guitar and vocal. This is not necessarily a rule, but an emulation of the way the majority of these types of records are mixed. With this low-endy EQ on the bass (leaving out a lot of the mids during the rhythm parts of the song), the problem of emptiness is even more accentuated when the guitar player goes for a solo.

The way I'll usually deal with this problem is with a second bass guitar sound. The second sound will have a lot more mid frequencies and highs EQ'd into it than the main bass sound. This can come from a variety of places. One way is to use a microphone on the bass guitar speakers to get a little more chunk than the main DI gives you. I have also added a channel from the pre-amp output on the back of the bass amp and then boosted some EQ on the console if needed. A new way (and probably the best way) to accomplish this seems to be Y-cabling the main bass source sound into two channels on the board, and then EQ'ing the second channel with more mids and highs and maybe some cut in the low end. What you now have is a rhythm bass as opposed to a rhythm guitar to fill in during the solos. This could be accomplished with just changing EQ on the bass during the solos but if you have the channels on the board to spare I suggest this for ease, speed and consistency.

Using this method will help you to have plenty of space in the mix during the rhythm parts for a big, fat, uncluttered guitar, and a full frequency range for vocal, without the bass fighting for those mids. When the guitar player goes for a solo, the chunky mid frequencies of the bass are there to make the musicians sound fuller than the three-piece band they are. If the band desires a fuller frequency bass sound throughout the entire song, this second sound can double as an optional tone to add in or not. However, if they are looking to feature the guitar sound and leave the bass more for fullness and foundation, then give this method a try.

One reason I believe the "Y" method to be the most effective is that you don't have to worry too much about phase cancellation. When you have the same source going into two channels instead of a couple of different sources (e.g. DI and mic), your chances for phase consistency are much better. Give this a try, it has shown itself to be very valuable tool for me.

"MIC TECHNIQUES"

6/12/99 Luis Miguel

The way a singer moves on and off the capsule of the mic when he or she sings is known as mic technique. I believe that quality mic technique starts with keeping a reasonably close distance between the lips and the mic for most of the performance, controlling the level going into the mic by changing distance from the mic to do so. Sounds easy, doesn't it?

Let me start by saying I am not a singer, as will be attested by anyone who knows me well, so my understanding from a performer's standpoint of how to work the mic is not as good as it could be. But from a sound engineer's standpoint, I hope to have the technique described above used by the singers I work with. The positive result of using good mic technique is this: If the singer works the mic properly, the volume of the vocal passage being performed can be controlled by the performer. If a part of the performance is very soft, the singer can move right onto the capsule of the mic and help raise the level coming out. If the note being sung is very loud, moving off the mic can help control the level, to a certain extent.

The experienced sound engineer knows that when you move closer to the capsule of most vocal mics, dynamic or condenser, a process known as proximity effect happens, which boosts the low-end frequencies. As you move away from the mic, the overall level drops considerably, but the low end diminishes at a more severe rate.

Herein lies the problem, and I'm going to suggest a few ways to control this. First, use a compressor. Compressing a vocalist's mic channel will help with the drastic level changes that occur.

Second, use a dynamic equalizer. There are several brands, but the one I have used extensively is a BSS unit called the DPR-901. Its function is to compress, but in a manner based on a selected frequency range you choose, similar to a parametric EQ. It's a great unit, but tricky to master.

I like to put the dynamic EQ in my insert chain first, and follow that up with a parametric EQ to further control things and diminish the problem frequency range first, before compressing the whole vocal level. Why not just use the dynamic EQ? Because it doesn't always do the whole job, and as I mentioned before, it's tricky to master.

Third, and this is not always a viable option, talk to your singer and explain the problem you are having with her moving too far off the mic. The problem is that when the singer sings 75 percent of the time from a distance of four inches or more from the mic, you are forced to add low end to the channel EQ. After you've done this, a thunderous explosion will happen when they finally do get right on the mic and belt out something with lots of low-end content. This wasn't as much of a problem for me when I worked more with rock 'n' roll acts because the singers had to be right on the mic to hear themselves, so the fluctuations were less. But what I've found with artists who sing lighter styles of music is that they move in and out of range of the mic's proximity effect a lot, so the need to manually control tonality is much greater.

The toughest thing about all of this is the inconsistency of results. In a reasonably dead acoustic environment, you may not notice this problem as much, but in a big boomy room with a concert-size PA, the added low end from the singer jumping all over the mic capsule will really be a big deal.

I find that I change my methods from day to day and venue to venue. Sometimes I lean more toward dynamic EQ, sometimes it's more standard compression, and sometimes I kick both of these tools out of the insert chain and just ride the vocal fader up and down manually. A fourth suggestion, one that started to work really well for me about a week after first writing this, is setting up the low frequency on a parametric EQ (either on the channel EQ or outboard) for a maximum bandwidth cut at a center frequency around 60 Hz. It takes a lot of babysitting to control the pops and thumps of low end, but if you get to know where the singer is going to jump on the mic, you can ride the knob up and down to compensate for these low-end bursts.

In the end, if you are able, talk to your singer and explain what is happening. If you can demonstrate the effect of proximity on the mic with the PA on, great! Your singer may not understand fully what he's doing to the sound out front by moving on and off the mic. In this day of in-ear monitors, the difference between a couple of inches may not be severe in the head of the singer, but out front it can be substantial. Sometimes a board tape of the show may be enough to get the singer pondering why the tone of his voice keeps changing.

If you have a conversational relationship with your singer and you feel you can alter his or her habits by chatting about it, go for it! But beware, it may be taken the wrong way and make you look like you're overstepping your bounds as the sound engineer. Also, be sure to try several microphones (again, if your singer is game for a mic switch), and see what works best. I'm crazy about the vocal aspect of mixing. I think it's extremely important and should be pursued with diligence. We can't always control what goes in, but we can do our best to have it come out right.

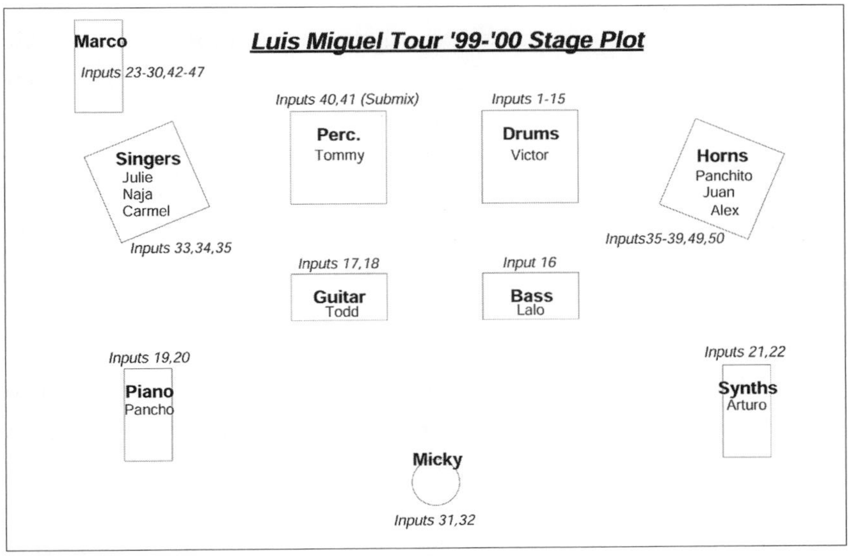

A handy item to have around, a stage plot is great to send to people you might be working with soon, like a local sound company. It acts as a clear picture of the layout of your stage.

"TIMING IS EVERYTHING"

2/20/98 Van Halen

Have you ever made a recording of the show and blended in a stereo microphone or a couple of microphones in the house to liven up the board mix a little? You may find that if you place the mics quite a ways back in the house (at the mix position, for example), the tape may sound very confusing and boomy. One reason is that the mic is hearing things a good 100 feet or more later than the board feed, depending on how far from the speakers you are.

Some live recordings will go for this "out of time" room microphone sound to make the mix sound more live, and this is okay. But if you are having trouble with boomy recordings, the quick fix is to delay the console feed to the recording device by the distance you are from the speakers, multiplied by .8965 (See "If you've got the speakers, I've got the time," page 95).

You can also use a computer delay location program like Smaart or SIM to calculate the distance more accurately.

Sound complicated? Well, it really isn't. On one tour I had a little outboard Mackie mixer that I would use to take the record feed from my console (which ran through a digital delay unit) and also an input from a stereo microphone. The digital delay would delay the console to line up with the mic and then the Mackie output would feed the recording DAT deck. My board tapes sounded better that ever. Give it a try.

Another cool thing to do—this is definitely a luxury—is to delay the PFL feed to your headphones by the amount of time you are away from the speakers. It can be really frustrating at times to cue up the kick drum and hear the attack of the drum in the headphones some 150ms before the sound from the speakers gets to your ears. This takes a bit of wiring, but usually you can figure out a way to do it. This same process has become a staple for me with my console monitors. If you have the time and a spare delay in the rig that you travel with or use all the time, you will love the results.

These things are not always easy to do when you're doing one-offs, but if you are preparing a system for a long tour or you use the same console and effects/processing racks all the time, you will love how spoiled you'll feel with these little extras.

"TRIGGER HAPPY"

2/27/98 Van Halen

Way, way back in the forgotten era of mid-eighties rock 'n' roll and highly polished pop music, there was a trend in our industry to use drum samples to substitute for what everyone considered boring and stale acoustic drum sounds. That trend faded away and everyone started to realize that good old wood-shelled drums sounded pretty darn good if miked and tuned correctly.

One of the toughest things to overcome when we used sampled drums was getting the acoustic drum to trigger whatever sampler was delivering the drum sound. Many different variations of pads hit the market, but most drummers in the rock 'n' roll genre felt a little less than monstrous sitting behind a set of pads. From this testosterone-based need, the challenge was put forth to drum techs and sound engineers alike to find a trigger that would always open, even when hit lightly, yet not mis-trigger or double trigger. This had the manufacturers scurrying about, and some decent products hit the shelves. Some of these are still in use today, although the triggered/sampled drum sound has fallen out of favor.

With this in mind, I recently experimented with a concept that had been gnawing at me to try and found that it worked as well if not better than I had hoped. The idea was to use triggers on drums, but only for the purpose of opening drum noise gates and nothing more.

One drummer I work with is particularly adamant about open-sounding drums and hates to hear a gate open and close when he listens back to a board tape. Well, this is a daunting task when you are dealing with large drums, a large PA, and a high volume situation. I would find that the threshold to open the gates had to be so loose to allow those lightly struck drum parts to get through that as soon as the main part of the kit was being played, all the gates would open up at once. Another problem was that cymbals were constantly bleeding through the tom mics, and as we have all found, the EQ needed to make toms cut through can often make cymbals sound very brash and overwhelming.

The main objective was to get the tom gates to trigger by vibration rather than audio input. I tried several different triggers and found one made by a company called ddrum that worked especially well. It clamps over the edge of the drum rim and a little foam pad with a trigger on it rests ever so gently on the head of the drum. By sending this trigger (which just happens to have a very convenient and smartly designed XLR out) down the snake line and into the key input of my noise gates, I was able to get a much lower occurrence of false triggering than ever before.

The only thing that opens that tom mic now is vibration of the tom head. With a drummer playing 4/4 time at full throttle, I am now able to set the noise gates on the toms to stay shut, yet a very light tap on the tom head will open it up. It is a revelation. Can I get a hallelujah? The overheads are now able to be EQ'd the way you would like cymbals to sound, and they end up being the only mics that capture the cymbals.

A lot of drummers in rock 'n' roll consistently hit their drums hard, so gate thresholds may not be a problem for you. However, if you have a drummer who whacks his drums most of the time, but wants to play with some feel at other times, I would highly recommend this system. I tried it on kick drums and it just didn't seem to work as well as it did on the toms, so I stuck to just regular, light acoustic triggering. The snare is just a little too temperamental in some of the bands I've mixed, so up to this point I have not tried it there. Give it a try and see if you can finally be trigger happy.

CHAPTER 2

Note Taking

With manuals, documents, and text files on your computer or handheld device, there are a million ways to have data at your fingertips. The reason for this chapter is that I believe you absolutely should gather this information.

Learn model numbers of equipment, keep lists of microphones and mixing boards, and keep it handy. With the help of computers, it's so much easier to have this data close at hand. I know you dropped out of school to live a wild rock 'n' roll lifestyle, but you're still going to fail the test if you don't study or write a term paper.

"HE'S MAKIN' A LIST, AND CHECKIN' IT TWICE"

6/14/97 Ted Nugent

Knowledge is power, and the positive effects can begin with something as simple as not making a fool of yourself when you're ordering up equipment from the local sound provider for an upcoming show.

It can make you appear wildly unprofessional when you put things in your equipment spec that read like this: "(8) Aphex noise gates (the new ones, I can't remember the model number)."

I picked this particular example because every time I would go to spec out this Aphex noise gate I could never find the ad in one of my sound mags, and for the life of me I could never remember that model number. The lesson we should all be learning is that having a good, thorough, and updated list of various types of equipment we work with all the time will help you to put a professional spec sheet together, at least for those times when you have the option of picking what gear you would like to use at a show.

It will also help you when a club owner is asking you if you would like "this" piece of gear instead of "that" one and it's important to give him quick and accurate answers. Getting a model number on a compressor wrong by one or two numbers can mean you get four mono compressors (four total), instead of the four quad compressors (for a total of 16) that you need to do the show properly. I keep my list right in my phonebook/organizer so that as I'm making calls, if the situation arises that I need to pull a model number out of the hat, I can appear to professionally have it all together. As you're reading sound mags or equipment brochures, jot down the model numbers and a brief description of what that piece of equipment does and slowly build a library. Knowledge is power, but data begets knowledge.

"LEARN THE TOOLS OF THE TRADE"

6/15/94 Ted Nugent

It's easy to get into an audio rut using the same club PA with the same band week after week without ever getting a chance to play around with other gear. Don't get me wrong; there's a lot to be said for becoming the master of a certain effects unit or piece of processing gear and using it to its fullest capabilities. If this is all you are able to get your hands on for the time being, forge ahead with that trusty, steadfast gear and do all you can with it. But if chances come along to try out a new reverb unit or crossover system for your PA, I suggest you borrow that piece of gear and spend a little time with it.

The more pieces of equipment you are familiar with, the better equipped you will be when you find yourself mixing on unfamiliar gear in a one-off situation. Even having a good look over a mixing board that someone else is using, to familiarize yourself with the routing and functions, will better prepare you for that pressure-cooker situation. I would also suggest making lists and charts of the gear you now know, and list details about the gear so you can recognize what you are looking for when you put a spec together. A great example of this is having a mic list that specifies whether the mic is a condenser, dynamic or specialty mic. Describing the tonal qualities of various mics and listing where those mics are best used will help you immensely when you are trying to spec a show with a sound company, promoter, or club owner.

You will find that you can't always get your favorite mics, and having this list will give you an option for another mic if your favorite isn't available. Knowing what would be the best alternative is not always the easiest of tasks when simply recalling choices from memory. Even if you haven't used a certain mic before, ask an engineer who is currently using one to share the wealth and tell you what's good and bad about it and document this.

Also, when you have one hour to do a soundcheck on unfamiliar gear, it's good to have some notes on the programming functions of a not-so-common or recently used effects unit. It's not easy to get a hold of every manual for every piece of gear out there, and not at all easy to lug them around with you all the time. Fortunately, with the recent advent of Internet web sites much of this can be downloaded quite quickly in a pinch. This is not always available to you, however, so spend as much time as you can with unfamiliar equipment and be a master of the tools of our trade.

A list of general microphone properties will help you decide what to try when you are looking for a change, and will give you a good list to choose from when you are trying to put an equipment spec list together for a show.

<u>Microphone Properties List: (*Excerpt*)</u>

<u>Shure:</u>

SM 57-

- Dynamic cardoid
- Good all round instrument and sometimes vocal mic
- Great for electric guitar and drums
- Dark gray with black vented windscreen

SM 81-

- Pencil condenser
- Good for hi-hat and cymbals, acoustic guitar
- Three position Gain Pad
- Three position High Pass
- Silver color

SM/Beta 91-

- Condenser "boundary/plate" mic
- Great for kick drum (tight low end and sharp attack)
- Separate power supply with high pass and pad switches
- 3" x 4" flat square black plate with black flat screen

<u>Audio Technica:</u>

ATM 23-

- Dynamic Cardoid
- Great for snare and toms (use in place of SM 57)
- All purpose instrument mic
- Grey vented finish, about the size of pill bottle

AT 4041-

- Pencil Condenser
- Hi-hat and cymbals, acoustic guitar
- Black with slotted top

AT 4054-

- Condenser, cardoid
- Smooth response, high output, vocal mic
- Built-in 80Hz roll-off
- Black finish with black windscreen

AT 4055-

- Condenser, cardoid
- Same properties as 4054 but no 80 Hz roll-off
- Great full bodied kick drum mic
- Same appearance as 4054 (look closely at color of ring around windscreen)

A list of general microphone properties will help you decide what to try when you are looking for a change, and will give you a good list to choose from when you are trying to put an equipment spec list together for a show.

5/27/94 Extreme

If you've been mixing a band or show for more than a couple of days on the same console, you will usually have your gain structure pretty much figured out. If you then find out that you'll be doing some one-offs in the near future on different mixing consoles, it's a good idea to chart your channel input gain settings and subgroup, VCA, and master levels. When you jump on another system, whether it's the same brand console or not, you can usually get things in the ballpark if you are faced with a very limited soundcheck, or none at all.

All that's left to figure out after this is the console's master output that will correspond with the drive gain of the system you're on. There will be days when you're doing a festival show or opening act slot and will be faced with no soundcheck. It's a real feeling of relief to step up to the plate and know at least the console input gains and some EQ and effects assignments are where they should be. Chart your home console's settings and don't leave home without them!

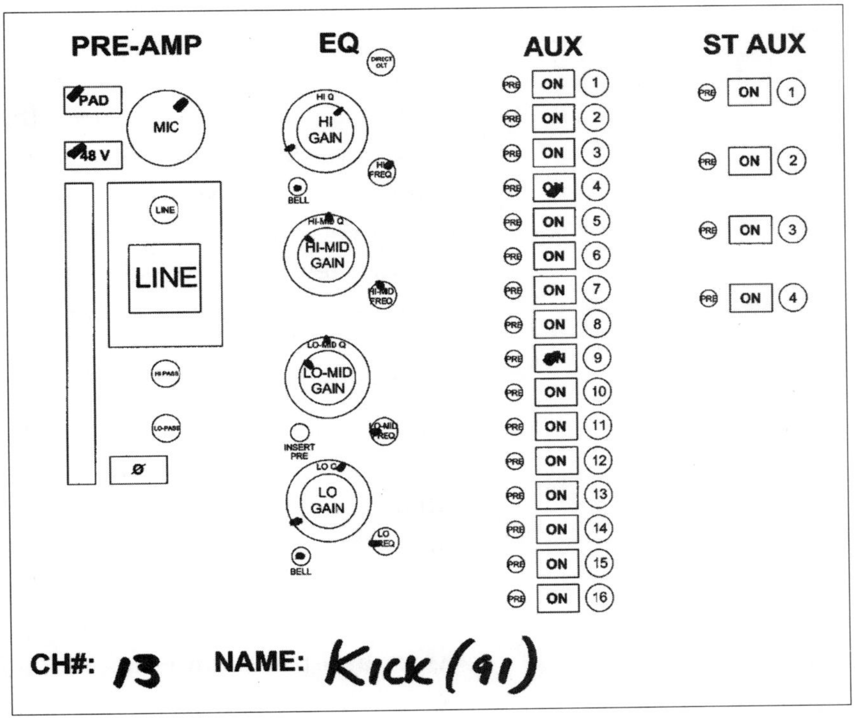

Console channel with settings filled in.

After you have a mix somewhat together on your console (after rehearsals or a few shows), jot down each channel's knob positions on your chart so you can transfer your mix to another console and PA when the time comes. This doesn't have to be a painstaking job, and just roughing it in on paper will be more than adequate to get you in the ballpark.

"A PENCIL AND A STENCIL"

5/28/93 Van Halen

A lot of things that go wrong when we go from the cozy world of regular touring to the one-off festival-style shows can be avoided with a little forethought and preparation.

We are all forced at one time or another to do a show that may have five or six bands on the bill. You will often find that two or three need to share the same mixing board and signal processing. One thing that happens when we are thrown from the comfort of our touring PA, and stuck on some unfamiliar, unmerciful mixing console, is that at soundcheck we may only get a short time to get a few sounds and not much more.

If the next band to soundcheck is to follow shortly, there may not be much time to jot down the settings you dialed in during your line check. If you only have a very short time, you may only get to chart your input gain settings and leave it at that. But if you have a few more minutes it is really helpful to jot down a few of the EQ settings and other important channel input settings you feel are worthy.

To help you do this so it doesn't end up looking like chicken scratch, make a stencil drawing of the console's input channel layout and have some copies around. I said earlier that you sometimes find yourself on a console you've never used before. In these situations, chicken scratch is sometimes all you have time for. But when you work on a console for a while and you have some free time to look it over, get out a ruler and pencil and make up a stencil of what an input channel looks like and keep that with you for a rainy day. This is also a great idea for signal processing gear like gates and compressors so that after a quick line check you can chart where your gate and comp settings ended up. This goes for EQs too.

You can make these as simple or as detailed as you like, but to have a folder of stencils for the various pieces of gear you encounter will be sure to come in handy. I have gone about making drawings of various pieces of gear on my computer over the years. If I have enough time to prepare for these tight time constraints, I will print out a couple of copies of signal processor templates for the gear I will be setting during soundcheck, and a bunch of console input drawings (as many as you need to chart the console, and some spares).

Trust me, you will be "the man" when the previous band finishes and you step up to the plate armed with paper in hand. You twist knobs, you set gains, and you are a hero who will hear the glory of your brilliance as your band's set starts and they sound like angels sent from heaven. Of course, the crowd will cheer your Midas touch. Well, maybe not, but you will feel the pride of a job well done. And that's sometimes enough. Well, OK, getting paid helps too.

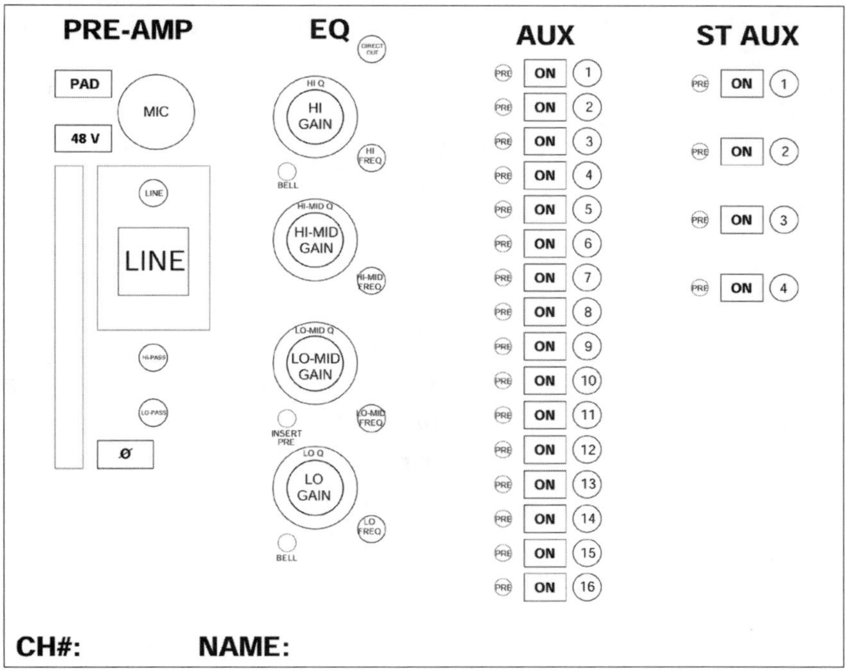

Console channel template.

Print as many of these out as you have console channels and fill them in. Update them every month or so. I use a sharpie marker and "rough it in;" it's more of a security blanket than anything. It can be a lifesaver if someone rubs their arm across your console and wipes out your lead vocalist's channel settings.

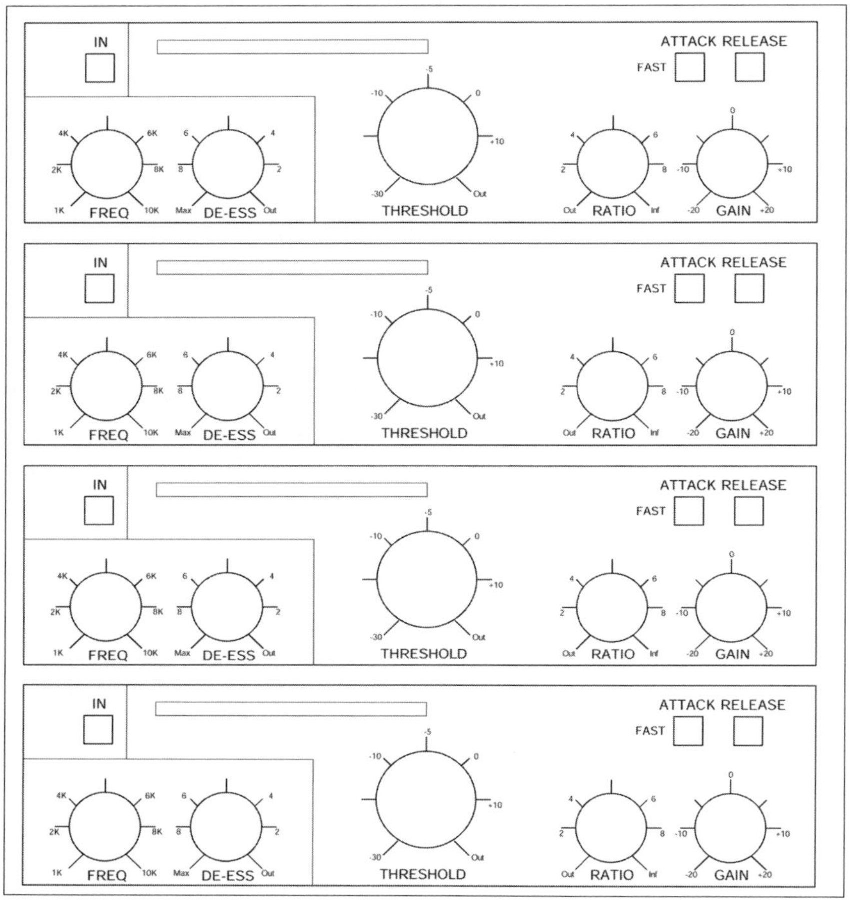

This is an example of a blank template to use in documenting knob settings on a BSS DPR-404 quad compressor. When you are involved in a multi-act show and everyone is using the same processing gear, jotting down your comp settings after soundcheck and resetting them right before your show will give you so much more confidence and a much tighter start to your show.

5/18/93 Van Halen

This goes hand in hand with the last memo. It's a great idea to keep your effects settings logged and recorded for easy recall. If it's one of the newer effects units, it may have a slot for a disk of some sort where you can simply download all your preset reverb, delay and assorted effects to the disk. This way you can have that disk ready to load into the same unit when it appears in a rack at a one-off near you, or when you use a different PA rental.

These disks can also travel with you from tour to tour and from act to act so that in a pinch you can call up good old snare reverb #25 and know you have something that has worked for you in the past. What I have done when using units that don't have a way of storing the memory to disk, is create a logbook of various effects units with my favorite preset settings. If I do a show where the sound company is providing some of the old familiar units we all know, I can be sure to whip up some settings I'm familiar with, without having to spend all afternoon with a mic and headphones trying to get some decent sounding reverbs.

As with the above memo, you don't always have time to put on the headphones and program presets anyway. I'm not much of a fan of just going to default program #1 and hoping it sounds good. Having your favorite settings on paper will help immensely. Another helpful hint is to always store your programs in the same memory number. When I do a show where other sound engineers will be sharing the effects units, I like to try to get with them at soundcheck and reserve a certain bank of numbers to store my programs. I always go from 75 to 85 (for some strange, habitual reason).

The important thing is, if you get with the other guys early enough, you can help ensure that you won't spend hours programming effects only to have someone jump all over your program numbers and put their own there. These timesaving tips will help you start a show off with the paperwork already done and leave you free to concentrate on the mixing part.

FX PROGRAMMING CHART

PGM #	SONG	PCM 70 Horn Reverb	H-3000 BG Voc Harm.,etc	SPX 990 #1 Misc. Uses	SPX 990 #2 BG Voc Reverb	TC 2290 Micky Voc Delay	PCM 80 Drum/Perc Reverb	480 Machine 1B Fat Snare/Mickey Sp	EMT 250 Micky Verb
1	PRE-SHOW								
2	Tu Mirada						LM Snare	LM EMT Long	2.0 Seconds
3	Sol Arena Y Mar	Long Hall Horn	Layered Shift		Thin Verb		Short Snare (Inv)		1.5 Seconds
4	Tu Solo Tu	Long Hall Horn	Layered Shift		Thin Verb		Short Snare (Inv)		1.5 Seconds
5	Te Propongo	Long Hall Horn	Layered Shift	On the Phone-LM	Thin Verb		Short Snare (Inv)		1.5 Seconds
6	O Tu O Ninguna	Med Warm					LM Snare	LM EMT Long	2.0 Seconds
7	Quiero	Long Hall Horn	Dual Shift	Sax solo Plate	Thin Verb		Short Snare (Inv)		1.5 Seconds
8	Soy Yo						LM Snare		
9	No me Fio						LM Snare		
10	No me Platiques Mas			Sax solo Plate			LM Snare	LM EMT Long	2.0 Seconds
11	No Se Tu						LM Snare	LM EMT Long	2.0 Seconds
12	La Puerta						LM Snare	LM EMT Long	2.0 Seconds
13	La Barca		Stereo Shift		Fat Verb		LM Snare	LM EMT Long	2.0 Seconds
14	Inolvidable	Long Hall Horn	Dual Shift		Thin Verb		LM Snare	LM EMT Long	2.0 Seconds
15	Intro								
16	Bass Solo			Fretless Solo-Bass	Breathy Verb-Perc				
17	Dormir Contigo						LM Snare	LM EMT Long	2.0 Seconds
18	Ese Momento						LM Snare		
19									
20	El Dia Que me Quieras	Med Warm					LM Snare	LM EMT Long	2.0 Seconds
21	Solamente una Vez						LM Snare	LM EMT Long	2.0 Seconds
22	Somos Novios						LM Snare	LM EMT Long	2.0 Seconds
23	Todo Y Nada						LM Snare	LM EMT Long	2.0 Seconds
24	Nosotros	Long Hall Horn		Sax solo Plate			LM Snare	LM EMT Long	2.0 Seconds
25									
26									
27									
28									
29									
30	Voy a Apagar la Luz						LM Snare	LM EMT Long	2.0 Seconds
31	Contigo Aprendi						LM Snare	LM EMT Long	2.0 Seconds
32	Por Debajo de la Mesa						LM Snare	LM EMT Long	2.0 Seconds
33	Reloj						LM Snare	LM EMT Long	2.0 Seconds
34	Sabor a Mi	Long Hall Horn					LM Snare	LM EMT Long	2.0 Seconds
35	La Gloria eres Tu		Dual Shift		Echo Room Verb		LM Snare	LM EMT Long	2.0 Seconds
36	Besame Mucho	Long Hall Horn	Layered Shift		Thin Verb		LM Snare		1.5 Seconds
37	La Bakina	Med Warm	Layered Shift		Fat Verb		LM Snare		1.5 Seconds
38	Y	Med Warm					LM Snare		1.5 Seconds
39							LM Snare		
40	Un Hombre busca..mujer	Long Hall Horn			Chorus + Reverb	320 m/s (5 fdbck)	LM Snare		1.5 Seconds
41	Cuestion de Piel	Long Hall Horn	1200m/s Micky Dly		Chorus + Reverb	300 m/s (20 fdbck)	LM Snare		1.5 Seconds
42	Oro de Ley	Long Hall Horn	Layered Shift	Sax solo Plate	Fat Verb	282 m/s (20 fdbck)	Short Snare (Inv)		1.5 Seconds
43									
44									
45									
46	Que tu te Vas					469 m/s (20 fdbck)	Balad Verb	LM EMT Long	2.2 Seconds
47	Dame	Long Hall Horn	Layered Shift		Thin Verb	308 m/s (0 fdbck)	LM Snare		1.5 Seconds
48	Suave	Long Hall Horn	Layered Shift	Sax solo Plate	Fat Verb		Short Snare (Inv)		1.5 Seconds
49	Como es Posible	Long Hall Horn	Layered Shift	Flange-LM	Thin Verb	530 m/s (20 fdbck)	LM Snare		1.5 Seconds
50	Sera Que No me Amas	Long Hall Horn	Layered Shift		Fat Verb		LM Snare		1.5 Seconds

Effects programming chart.

With all the data storage capabilities available today, it's still not always possible to store every parameter on a floppy or RAM card. When you can't point and click, pick up a pen and jot them down. You'll find yourself needing those parameters sometime during the tour (someone else's PA on a one-off, or a reverb unit that dies), and you'll be glad when you come back next year that you stored all that data.

DELAY/HARMONIZER CHART FOR VH-III

	DELAY	HARMONIZ ('Dual Shift) Pitch/Delay/Fbk
WITHOUT YOU	640/680	-13/13/0
FIRE IN THE HOLE	620/310	-13/0/20
HOW MANY SAY I	640/680	-13/13/10
ONCE	820/410	-14/15/13
JOSEPHINA	660/340	-12/13/10
ONE I WANT	458/402 (manual record) (610/310) (Tempo of song) ?.	-13/13/0
FROM AFAR	330/660	-13/15/20
DIRTY WATER DOG	200/400	-11/13/7
BALLOT OR THE BULLET	300/600	-13/13/10
A YEAR TO THE DAY	640/320	-13/13/15

Delay Pan

L R

How do you ensure you're going to make that cool effect from the CD sound just right on tour? Ask the guy who mixed the record what effects and what setting he used. These settings were given to me by Van Halen's studio engineer on VH III. Thanks Robs!

FX Parameters

PCM 70 (Horns)-

Long Hall Horn-
Page:

0			1	RT Low	1.4 s	2	Diffusion	45
0.1	FX Adj.	5 dB	1.1	RT Mid	1.4 s	2.1	Attack	30
0.2	Soft Knob	0	1.2	X-Over	2.27 kHz	2.2	Definition	19
0.3	Size	38.3 m	1.3	RT HC	7.47 kHz			
0.4	Gate	Off	1.4	RTL Stop	2.7 s			
0.5	Pre Delay	16 ms	1.5	RTM Stop	2.3 s			
0.6	H Cut	4.85 kHz						
0.7	Decay Op.	On						
0.8	Chorusing	50						

LM Med Warm-
Page:

0			1	RT Low	.74 s	2	Diffusion	60
0.1	FX Adj.	0 dB	1.1	RT Mid	.61 s	2.1	Attack	42
0.2	Soft Knob	0	1.2	X-Over	1.12 kHz	2.2	Definition	30
0.3	Size	12.0 m	1.3	RT HC	7.47 kHz			
0.4	Gate	Off	1.4	RTL Stop	.91 s			
0.5	Pre Delay	12 ms	1.5	RTM Stop	.91 s			
0.6	H Cut	6.83 kHz						
0.7	Decay Op.	On						
0.8								

H-3000 (BG VOCALS)-

Dual Shift-		Orig Pgr. #102		
	Left Fine	5 cents	Right Fine	5 cents
	Left Delay	25 ms	Right Delay	25 ms
	Left Fdbck	0%	Right Fdbck	0%
Layered Shift-		Orig Pgr. #101		
	Left Fine	12 cents	Right Fine	12 cents
	Left Delay	25 ms	Right Delay	25 ms
	Left Fdbck	0%	Right Fdbck	0%
Stereo Shift-		Orig Pgr. #103		
	Fine	6 cents		
	L & R Delay	25ms		
	Fbck	0%		

Long Digiplex-		Orig Pgr. #109
Song #41	Delay	1200 ms
	Fbck	0%

SPX 990 #1 (Special FX)-

Sax Solo Plate- Orig Pgr. #2 (St. Rev)
Page:

1	Rev Type	Vocal				
2	Rev Time	1.9s	Hi Ratio	0.8	Ini Delay	44.5
3	Inp Mix	4	Crs Dly	18	ER/Rev	64
4	Density	4	LPF	10k		
5	On/Off	On	Balance	100%		

On The Phone- Orig Pgr. #75 (Echo)
*No Parameters Changed

A simple list of effects parameters and program numbers to keep on record.

Program numbers and FX Parameters for VH III Tour

PGM #	SONG	DELAY (ms)	SPECIAL Fx	
1	Right Now	675		
2	Unchained	200		
3	Without You	640-------------	[Leslie Simulator]	
4	One I Want	610		
5	When it's love	300		
6	Ballot or the Bullet	600		
7	Why Can't this be Love	300		
8	Romeo Delight	200		
9	Dreams	300		
10	Dirty Water Dog	400		
11	Runnin with the Devil	200		
12	Humans Being	480-------------	[Spx 990 Dual Flange	
13	Year to the Day	640	Mod Freq-.5	Phase-90
14	Mean Street	200	Depth 1-100	2-100
15	Ain't Talkin bout Love	200	Delay 1-2.1	2-2.5
16	How Many Say I	0	FB Gain-99	Mode-ST]
17	Jump	200		
18	Fire in the Hole	620-------------	[Reverse Verb on BG]	
19	I'm the One	200		
20	Somebody/Doctor	200		
34	You Really Got Me	200		
35	Dance the Night Away	200		
36	Poundcake	275		
37	Panama	0		
38	From Afar	660		
39	Once	820		
40	Josephina	660-------------	[Spx 990 #1	Spx 990 #2
			Delay L,C,R	Dual Pitch
			L Delay-310	Pitch-Unison
			R Delay-620	Fine (1) +9
			FB 1-100	Fine (2) -9
			FB 2-200	Delay (1)-10
				Delay (2)-20]

This is another example of a simple effects program list that includes the program number, song title, delay time, and special effect that might happen in that song.

"DO IT BY THE BOOK"

5/90 Aerosmith

Have you ever found yourself jotting down notes on your nightly set list to remind yourself that "song A" needs this type of delay, and "song B" needs the keyboards turned up, and in "song C" you need to mute all the background vocals?

Well, after a while you may find that you keep losing that one sheet of paper with all your vital cues on it or it may get too crumpled to read. For this reason I started a project in 1990 that I have continued to this day, and have found it works really well. I acquired a little six-ring binder book that is no larger than four by six inches in size and this became my show cue book.

Every song in the show gets a page in the notes telling me who is doing the guitar or key solo, what effects are being used, any level changes that need to be made, and anything else that will help to remind me of things I couldn't possibly remember every night. The nice thing about having this type of book is that as the band changes the song order around you can simply open up the book and shuffle around the pages to get the songs in the right order. Other types of notepaper like flash card books can be torn from the binder and shuffled around, but when I first used this type of system I found myself dropping the book or losing certain pages and it just didn't work as well as the ring binder method.

Another tip is to use colored Sharpies and highlighter pens to label your book. For me, background vocal cues are always in red sharpie and drum cues (such as a note to let me know a song has a sidestick cue) are done in blue ink with green highlight. With the ability to link up effects with MIDI I also have a program number for each song and that is always in red ink at the top right of the page. By developing a page setup you will always recognize what type of cue is coming by your own repetitive system.

Another great benefit of this is if you find yourself going back a year later to a band to do another tour. You may not have the time to program all the effects again or listen to all the songs on the tapes, but you will have your notes to initially fall back on. If there are two guitar players it is so important to know who is going to do the guitar solos or which one starts the song. If the singers take turns singing lead, have a note describing who is singing in each song. Having your old notes around will help you immensely.

If you are changing your effects with MIDI, make sure you jot down all the effects settings and delay times in your book so that you can easily recall them if you use other gear or you return later with a new system. You might want to make a separate sheet with effects parameters to keep your cue sheet uncluttered. A lot of device manufacturers also give you the option of saving presets to various types of memory cards which is handy and fast, but I still recommend good old paper and pen for safety's sake. Make your cue notes clear and precise and do it by the book.

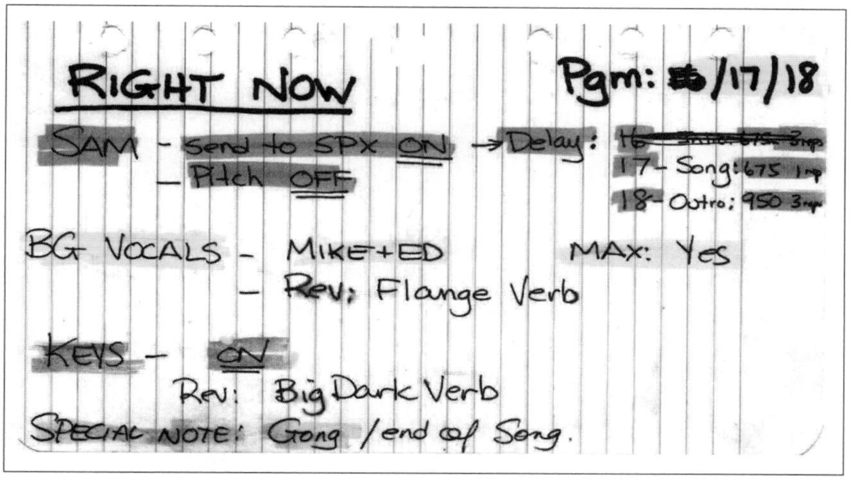

A good example of the types of key words that I use to clearly instruct myself in executing effects changes and mix moves in the heat of battle.

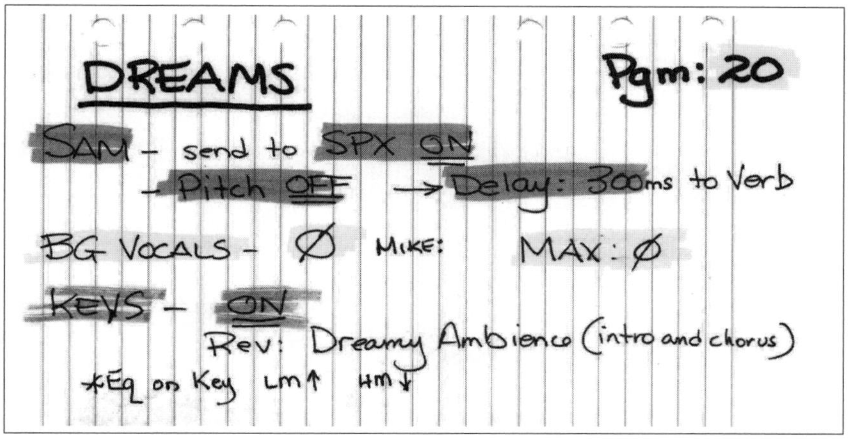

More of the same. Note the order of the commands. I like to follow the same lineup with each song and arrange the commands in order of most important to least, and also have them listed in the order they occur in the song.

CHAPTER 3

Mic Selection

I've heard it said many times that the mic is the most important element in the audio path because it's the first thing to come in contact with the sound being created. Well, we might have a lengthy debate over that one, but suffice it to say that choosing quality microphones is extremely important. As important as the mics you choose are the skills involved with mic placement and technique. Here are a few tips to improve your chops and a few options you might not have considered before. Happy miking.

"LIKE THEY ALWAYS SAY, 'MORE IS MORE'"

7/18/95 Van Halen

It's really easy in this business to overdo it and use every tool and device available to completely botch the whole thing up. They always say "less is more," and a lot of the time it is, but from time to time it can be very beneficial to add a little extra trick to reach a sum greater than the parts.

One such situation is to use more than one kick drum mic. There are a few reasons for this. Some rooms react to low end better or differently than others do. Sometimes a mic that sounded great in one room is just the wrong one for the next night's room.

Having more than one mic gives you the option of choosing the one that is sounding better in the situation you are in. I like to choose two mics (or even three sometimes) to give me these options. I also like them to sound quite a bit different from each other.

The next reason for going with the overkill method is to have a spare mic should one decide to take a dive during the show.

Have you ever been to a show where the kick drum mic decided to quit? Trust me, it's not a pretty place to be. It feels like Godzilla has just left the building.

This third reason is the inspiration for this memo: combining the different tones of the mics to get a better overall sound is a great trick. And the trick within the trick is in the EQ.

On a recent tour, I tried an approach I read about in *Mix* magazine used by a studio engineer who made a whole bunch of cash by being the Guru of Dance Mix tunes. He described a method of EQ'ing the two kick mics to hit you in a different place in relation to the feel of the low end. We have all felt the "super subby" kind of kick drum that is tuned and EQ'd very low (about 40 Hz is a rough center frequency for this example). And I'm sure you have also felt the kind of power you experience from the chest-kicking kick drum (tuned and EQ'd at about 60 to 80 Hz).

They each have their own effect, and as you listen to CDs or different engineers' mixes, you will sense that the producer/engineer is going for one or the other of these. A cool thing happens when you EQ the mics to each handle one of these sounds. You can get the chest pound with the click on it from one mic and the super sub sound from the other mic, and then combine and blend the two to your tastes. You will find that you get a much more audible and powerful sound this way.

It may not work for every act, but I have recently begun using this and it works great for all the different types of bands I have worked with, and they vary in style quite a bit. Try this little trick out and then call the engineer from *Mix* magazine and thank him. (You can also mention that I gave him a plug so he'll dig me too.) If your one goal in life is to make your band sound as good as those insanely repetitive dance records, then you're well on your way. If this isn't your one goal in life, try it anyway. And as you stroll down the road of life remember: More is More!

7/10/98 Van Halen

Have you been challenged, like I have, by a drummer trying to achieve the elusive John Bonham kick drum sound?

Now, this is a glorious goal, but it can only be achieved through diligent mic selection and placement. Even then, it seems that something is always missing. Maybe that's just the magic of Bonham and the talented engineers that recorded his drum kit over the years.

One trick that I picked up by looking at old photos of his kit was to place a mic on the front head of the drum. It's best to try a variety of mics and experiment with how much low end to roll off the channel to combine nicely with the inside mic, if you choose to combine the sounds of the two mics.

You may want to mess around with delaying the time or flipping the phase of the inside mic to line up with the front head mic to see if that changes things for the better. This means inserting a delay along with the gate (via a chain insert out of the first unit's output into the second unit's input) in the insert loop, and while this might not always be feasible, the results can be surprising.

What I have found is that the drum sound is given a much rounder tonality with a little more natural mid-tone than when using only the inside mic. If you find a cool room reverb to add to this you may get somewhat close to that great Bonham kick sound. You may find that by leaving all the bottom end in the EQ you will get a great sound with just the front head mic, but I have found it to be a little too "tubby" and indirect sounding. The combination of the two has always served me best.

You may also find that this isn't at all the sound you're looking for to accompany the type of musical act you're working with. It isn't for everyone. Just keep in mind that if you are trying to get away from the click and the thud you get from an inside mic, this may get you on your way to a deeper, richer, and more natural sound. Give it a go. You may find even more drunken bar patrons screaming "Zeppelin!" from their seats.

"'Y' USE A SIDESTICK MIC?"

4/11/96 Julio Iglesias

It's a shame that really good drum chops often get missed because live sound engineers can't mic everything. How many times have you seen (not heard) a drummer wailing away on a cowbell, being enjoyed by no one but himself? The same problem also happens with a group of tiny cymbals that are not getting picked up by an overhead.

We can't always mic everything, and because of budgets and the necessity for speed at certain shows, we simply have to do the best we can. When you're putting a tour together for the road, though, it's nice to mic up the kit with the intention of capturing all the toys the drummer has.

One mic that I never used much before, but have recently discovered adds a lot of depth to my drum sound, is a sidestick mic. By "sidestick" I mean the process by which a drummer lays his stick inside the rim of the snare and hits the top of the rim on the other side of the drum. It's a very woody sound and is usually quite hard to pick up in its entirety with just the main snare mic.

To aid in amplifying this, it is helpful to have another mic that points towards the spot where the stick hits the rim. If it just isn't possible to free up a microphone to use for this, then another approach is to 'Y' the snare-top mic into two channels of the board and designate one as the sidestick mic. With this separate channel you can add some high-mid EQ, and maybe a little more level, to get those sidestick shots to really cut through. I like to add a deep haunting verb to this mic as well to really bring the sidestick shots to life.

You may have to ride the fader or use some muting cues to turn this mic on and off, as it will drastically color the sound of your snare drum if left hot all the time. Used wisely, however, it will really add some zest to your drum sound. Since everybody picks on drummers all the time, it is the least that sound engineers can do in a humanitarian spirit to let the drummers of the world be heard.

7/01/93 Van Halen

A lot of sound engineers have to get by with a very limited arsenal of microphones. But there are also the lucky ones who have an almost unlimited supply of choices that they can try for various applications. Everyone has a favorite mic, but when you're in a time pinch or a situation where only the most basic mics are available, the good old standards are a fine choice.

On the blissful occasions when you have production rehearsals or a chance to spend time experimenting with different mics on an instrument, by all means check out some options.

I like to start with the mic I believe will work best and then set up a test mic in a similar position on that instrument and put it in an open channel on my mixing board. By switching back and forth between the two mics you can make a decision as to whether that mic is right in this situation.

The main message here is, never stop experimenting with mic choices in varying situations. Also, don't assume that a mic that worked well on guitar for one band will be the best choice for guitar with the next band you mix. Of course there are certain industry standards that are best suited for guitar, but try something different.

I've had situations arise where I was halfway into a tour and the musician walked in with a new microphone and asked me to try it out. With great apprehension (and knowing full well I couldn't say no), I did. Sometimes I would be pleasantly surprised and sometimes the results were unimpressive.

The important thing is, try. You never know when you'll stumble upon something that makes a dramatic difference. Some things must be considered, however. Cost has a lot to do with this, as does reliability on the road. A great sounding mic can give up and die at the first sign of heat or moisture or one good whack with a drum stick, so consider this as well. Be adventurous and go looking.

4/10/93 Van Halen

Life is full of choices, and whenever I'm given the chance I like to have as many as possible.

One of the only places on stage where it's possible to have a number of different choices of microphones is the kick drum. Because of the fact that the drum is rather large, a microphone stuck inside it is not in much danger of being whacked by a drumstick. You can even get away with putting a couple of mics in there. If you have enough open channels to go this way, I strongly suggest that you do this.

There are a few good reasons to indulge in more than one mic in the kick. One reason is, not all mics will give you the same sound, and I've found that a mic that sounded great in the kick one day may not be the best choice in a different room the next day. You can go ahead and try different mics every day and experiment until you find the best one for that particular room, but I can almost guarantee that the monitor engineer or audio tech that have to do all the switching and placing of mics, not to mention the EQ'ing, will probably suggest you find a place for the mic and move on. (I'm sure they'll have a suggestion for a place to put it that you might not want to try).

For this reason, I have a few different choices of mics that generally work in most drums with the least amount of EQ, and from the start of the tour I will decide on two or maybe three of them, and assign them to the input list from the get-go. With this rule of thumb, the monitor guy can pick the one that suits him the best and never use the others. This gives me the freedom every day to listen to several mics in each room and see which one works best for me, and never have to do a re-patch.

I will generally choose fairly different sounding mics. I like one that has a lot of low end in the frequency response and enough top end to make it work. Then I will choose another that has a tighter low end and maybe a little more mid and crack on top.

This gives me the option to change my mind depending on what the room is doing. If the room is very loose and sloppy in the low end, I will usually use the tighter sounding mic to give me more punch. If I'm mixing in an open air or extremely dead environment, then I will use the one with tons of "whomp" on the low end to help fill in the bottom.

Another reason for having two or more mics in the kick drum is the option of combining the sounds. Sometimes a mic that has a great low end has a real dead sounding top end, or the other way around. By combining the two mics, you can get the sound you're looking for without too much EQ.

Be warned, though, that the mics need to be placed at roughly the same distance from the head to avoid phase cancellation. As a rule of thumb, you should always move them around a little at first and pop the phase switch in and out to find the best combination.

Another good reason is the old "busted gear" syndrome. One of the toughest mics to get to, and one of the most missed in the mix should it stop working, is the kick mic. If a mic happens to give up the ghost during the show, it is great to have a backup ready and waiting. If you find a mic that has worked great for a while is getting upstaged day after day by another one of your selections, try swapping out the less popular one for an alternative. Be sure to keep in touch with your monitor guy to see which one he is using so that you don't take away something that is working for him and the band in the monitors.

Try to make the right choices during pre-tour rehearsals, but give new contenders a chance from time to time. You will often be surprised how good some of the new kick mics can sound, although I've often had the new great mic right alongside an old standard and found that from day to day the choice *du jour* would swap depending on the room. Like it or not, the kick drum always plays a pretty large role in the way your overall mix sounds and it's good to have choices. Exercise your right to choose.

CHAPTER 4

Rehearsals

Before my first "Big Rock" tour, I never would have believed the amount of rehearsing that goes into getting a show ready for the road. I remember thinking innocently that you run through the songs, figure out which ones run back-to-back, decide where the band was going to rap with the audience, and that was just about it. Well, I was wrong. I've spent anywhere from a month to two months getting ready for the first show of a tour.

It all happens in rehearsals. The band sees the stage and lights for the first time and figures out what stays and what goes. That goes for the crew as well. Many a good monitor guy has not made it through rehearsals. This is also the time to formulate an audio plan, build your rig, and fine-tune your wiring.

You will also get to know the songs painfully well during this time. I've spent many hours on my knees programming effects devices and have performed A/B tests on countless mics deciding which ones pass the test and make the tour.

Rehearsals aren't just for musicians anymore. We all get the time to be "show ready." Take advantage of every minute.

"YOUR MISSION, SHOULD YOU CHOOSE TO ACCEPT IT"

4/19/93 Van Halen

An open line of communication between the sound engineer and the band is a vital link to your success and continued employment. Knowing what the band is truly looking for is not always the easiest thing to pry from them in brief conversation or day-to-day soundchecking. Even so, you should always make it a priority to attempt to get a clear picture from the band as to what they are looking for.

One way to do this is with a question. Asking the band what album they would like to sound most like, or if they would like each song to be mixed in a way similar to the album it came from, is a good show of concern on your part.

You will often find that the band members themselves are not always in agreement with each other on the approach, but by the end of one meeting you can usually walk away with the answer you want. If the band says that the new album's sound is just the way they want it to sound live, then get a copy and go for sounds and effects that resemble the new album. I've even talked to the recording engineers to find out about an effect used on the album. I've received faxed parameters from these generous guys and this has helped immensely.

If the band wants each song to sound the way it did when it was recorded—even if that was ten years ago—you have a little more homework and effects programming ahead of you. One time, I incorporated this latter approach in the past and didn't check with the band first. About a month into rehearsals, I got a comment similar to "Oh, that record sounded terrible, don't make anything sound like that!"

Some bands will totally leave things in your hands, but getting things out in the open right from the get-go is a good policy. You may even find that they don't particularly like the way any of their records sound, and they will ask you to make them sound like a big-rock version of the rehearsal sessions. If the band you're mixing hasn't recorded yet, they may want you to study a certain artist's production on disk, and have you copy that. It's their choice, and it's your mission.

"BETWEEN A ROCK AND A SUB-BASS"

2/81 The clubs of western Canada

Phase cancellation and its disastrous effects can be painfully acquired bits of knowledge. One of the first lessons I ever learned as a fledgling sound apprentice was an easy way to check if two bass cabinets were in phase with each other. Before I ever knew what phase correctness was, a helpful sound engineer with considerably more talent than me offered to give my PA a listen, as I was not having much luck making anything sound good.

He taught me that the only way to achieve the volume and punch that a system was capable of putting out was to ensure that all the components were in correct phase. The testing of high-end drivers is a little bit more complicated that just strapping on a nine-volt battery and looking to see if the speaker cone jumps forward or sucks in, although this is a perfectly good way to test any paper-type cone speaker.

The simple wisdom I'd like to pass on merely requires you to run a little sound through your bass speakers and then get down in a crawling position and slowly move your head (with your ears attached) across the front of one speaker and then on to the front of the next speaker box. As you pass the area where the edges of the two speaker cabinets meet, you should notice one of two things: Either the level of bottom end that you're hearing will remain fairly constant, or it will drop dramatically in level. If this drop in level occurs, then the speakers in the two boxes you are listening to are out of phase with each other.

The little trick of attaching a nine-volt battery's positive and negative posts to the positive and negative posts of the speaker is one way to ensure all the cone drivers in your system are pushing the same way. However, this little trick of listening between the two bass cabinets (or midrange for that matter) is a real quick check when you suspect the system you are mixing on is sounding a little weak for how many speaker boxes there are. I learned this little lesson 19 years ago and I often use it for a quick check.

"I'VE GOT FEEDBACK ON THE BRAIN"

6/84 A club in Calgary, Alberta

If you want to be a mixer, you will need good ears. There are not many ways to train your ears aside from mixing, and you can't always do that. Something I did right at the start of my career that helped me more than I can ever know was to make a frequency tape.

Here's what I did: We finished playing in a hotel nightclub, and since we were staying in the same hotel the club owner would let us rehearse at low volume after everyone was gone. When the band was finished rehearsing and they had left, I stayed behind and set up to make my tape. I grabbed a vocal mic and a stand, and placed it about 20 feet in front of the PA stack at about midrange speaker height (five feet). I then went to the mixer and, after flattening my graphic equalizers, I brought the microphone up in the PA until it was just ready to feed back at a couple of frequencies. I also had another vocal mic back at the console for my own voice.

I then rolled a cassette tape on record and started by boosting a frequency on the graph until it began to feed back. I would let it ring for about three seconds and then bring it down and wait for another three seconds. I would then turn on my vocal mic (to tape only) and identify on tape the frequency boosted. The three seconds of silence after the boosted frequency gave me a chance to guess the frequency when I listened back to the tape. I continued with this procedure by boosting all the different frequencies along the graph. If you decide to give this a go, this tape will be your frequency identification practice tape that you can listen to anytime, anywhere.

You'll be surprised how much better your EQ'ing success will be on a PA after you spend some time with your tape. Make sure you make it long enough—45 minutes is a good length—or you can memorize a lot of the frequencies if your memory is fairly sharp.

People have asked me why I didn't just use a tone generator to duplicate this procedure. I'm sure you could, but anyone knows that real feedback is not exactly the same as a pure tone from a tone generator. Sometimes the feedback starts with a couple of frequencies in the same area taking off together, and then the one hot frequency will rise above and ring, and sometimes two frequencies will give you a kind of harmonic quality that a tone generator just can't copy. I used to test myself to see how many frequencies I would miss and this little self-competition made practice a little more enjoyable. I used this tape for years and it helped me considerably.

If you don't have access to a PA system to do this with you can probably rent or borrow one for an evening or even rent a studio to make it in. There are also CDs available now (like *The Mix Reference Disc,* published by Artistpro.com) that have a variety of listening tests and helpful test tones to use for trouble shooting and learning. The best ears will end up getting the biggest and best jobs in the end. Get your ears in shape.

PART TWO: LOAD IN

LOAD IN

You awake in your bunk, and your first thought should always be, "Thank God I'm not a lighting guy, I would have been up hours ago." You struggle to remember what city you've rolled into today and how many more shows until you get a day off. You know the toughest challenges that you may face all day are finding an open door into the venue and following the arrow signs to catering.

It's just another day on the road, and it's time to load in. Grab a cup of coffee and maybe a shower, and then hit the ground running. If you've been doing this for a while, you'll know the color of the seats in the arena before you ever see them, and you'll have a distinct memory of whether you love or hate this place. By the end of the day you may actually change your mind.

It's decision-making time. Where will you hang your speakers? How many do we really need to make it work? The choices you make now will shape your whole day.

Rub the sleep from your eyes and make that coffee a double. You know the words: "There's No Business Like Show Business..."

CHAPTER 5

Early Morning

The early bird gets the worm, and the lazy audio engineer gets stuck with his speakers hanging where the rigger decides they will hang. This is no time to be a "briefcase" engineer. There's no *i* in team, so join in and figure out where your PA is going. Walk the room, get a feel for the type of day you're about to have, and help shape that by meeting the important locals who will be a crucial part of making it great or not-so-great.

It's early, but this is an important time. *Carpe diem.*

"PAY ATTENTION TO THE HOUSE RULES"

7/05/97 Ted Nugent

Many tours that we do involve playing in different types of venues every night, with many different PA configurations. If you are traveling with a group that is only taking along band equipment, with sound and lights being picked up daily, you are one of the braver and luckier (that's right, the luckier) of the sound engineering establishment. This is because you will progress in skill and chops so much faster than the rest of us who are tweaking a knob or two every day and complaining that the drapes in the venue aren't thick enough.

With a different system every night, you will have good and bad nights, but you will learn a ton and become very proficient. If you have ever done this kind of tour, then you will probably agree with what I am about to say. My suggestion is to give the house sound guy a little bit of credit with his system before you go wiping out his house EQ curves and re-stacking his PA speakers. The reason I say this is that most house sound guys have been at their gig for at least a little while and have tried various configurations of stacking and flying the speakers they have to work with. They have also messed around with different EQ curves and settled on what they feel is best.

Now, this is not always the case. I have come into rooms where the sound guy has been gainfully employed by that establishment for eight days and has never mixed a drink, let alone a band. His closest contact to the world of audio may have been one conversation with another sound guy who gave him a tip or two (one of those being to try another line of employment).

The best way to check is to give the rig a listen. You can't start re-stacking the PA late in the day, so I suggest feeling out the house sound man's take on the stack and EQ and handing him your favorite CD when you first arrive. If the coverage is all off and the equalization sounds terrible, then nicely say you would rather do it your way if possible. Often you will find that where the system's parameters are set can turn out to be a good starting point. This will be a much kinder social interaction as well. No one likes to be pre-judged and looked down upon by someone else in our industry, but we so often give this appearance when we come into a room and pretend to know more about it than the guy who works there every day.

We may be miles ahead in skill level and experience, but as far as that room goes the house sound engineer may show you a thing or two. Ask him how the sections of the PA are divided up and what can be controlled and adjusted and what his concept of the room is. He will appreciate it and he will give you a valuable pointer nine times out of ten. If you pool all your resources you will have a better show and will gain his respect for allowing him to be heard. And having people say nice things about you and using all the benefits at hand to mix great sounding shows will keep you employed and requested. Give a listen first and give the locals a chance. You may be the house sound guy some day and you will appreciate the same considerations.

"IF YOU'RE HAPPY AND YOU KNOW IT, CLAP YOUR HANDS"

8/11/95 Van Halen

It's always kind of exciting to me every time I walk into a new venue and have a look around. So many of the places we play in have the same general architectural design and it's utterly amazing to me just how different two buildings that appear quite similar structurally can sound.

The summer-shed season is the most baffling of all to me. The outdoor amphitheaters that are spread all across North America have almost identical design formulas and a lot of the same materials are used to construct them, yet it is still a guessing game to predict the sound of the building. A little ritual that I do is to walk into the building in the morning and pay attention to the little noises that are going on around me. One of the best indicators of sonic quality is how clear and audible speech is from 50 feet away. I will pay attention in the morning to the riggers as they suspend the motor points in the ceiling and holler back and forth to one another.

If it is easy to understand someone speaking from the ceiling down to the ground from a good distance, it is probably going to be a decent sounding room, at least in the vocal clarity department. I always try to slam a couple case lids closed after I pull some cables out, because listening to how the slamming of a case lid excites the room can tell a lot about the reverb time and early reflection echoes.

One other trick that I use a lot is clapping my hands and having a listen. We can learn a lot by paying attention to how relatively quiet sounds reverberate around an empty room. The tough part is that we usually can't do much about it, but it may help you select how and where you will stack or fly your PA. By listening to the room unamplified, you can also prepare your ears for some of the weird things you might hear once you turn up a kick drum to 100 dB.

In short, pay attention in the a.m. for a more successful p.m.

PART THREE: SETUP

SETUP

This is the portion of the day that draws most from the pool of knowledge and motor skills you developed with a Lego set so many years ago. This is where it all comes together. The charge is always the same: "Put all of this stuff up in the air in a really short amount of time." Thankfully, you've done it a bunch of times already and it's like watching a team of robots build a car.

Once the decisions are made as to where your speakers are going to aim, how high you're going to fly them, and how many you're going to use, it's time to get them hanging and patched. My job recently has involved setting up front-of-house consoles and racks more than hanging speakers, so this is the time I'll patch it all together and get power flowing to it.

The other part of setting up that doesn't always get covered is the aspect of working with the clock, and working with others. It can really become an "It's all about me" situation at this time of day, as everyone is fighting for the same pieces of real estate for their gear. It often takes several chats with the Stage Manager to get it all worked out.

And it always does seem to work out, although not every department will be completely thrilled with the decisions. A speaker can't send sound through a light, and a light can't bend the beam around a speaker box. There will always be squabbles over a three-foot piece of stage. Whatever way the decisions go, what really matters is that the band will be on stage at 4 o'clock for a soundcheck, so get moving.

Could you remind me again why I didn't take a low stress job as a brain surgeon or air traffic controller?

CHAPTER 6

Setting up the System

If any of you have taken one or more of the fabulous audio measurement courses that are currently offered (SIM by Meyer, Smaart), you may have been surprised to discover the amount of time spent dealing with system design.

Before you learn to navigate the programs and incorporate keyboard shortcuts, and long before you start looking at data on your screen, you will be bombarded with lectures on the importance of designing and hanging your sound system correctly. I think some of us are a little offended by this. We think we have plenty of experience in this area and don't need to be schooled by a screen-watching "blip-counter."

The truth is, most of us have plenty to learn about placing speaker boxes in the most efficient configuration, and the popularity of these audio measurement programs has helped us see as well as hear the effects of proper placement. Usually, the choices are made in the design phase of production rehearsals, but there are always plenty of daily judgement calls to be made. For the average club sound mixer, you know the limitations placed on you by smaller numbers of speakers and processing force you into making great placement choices to achieve the best results.

These memos are some tips to help you decide how to array and locate your transducers to get the most bang for the buck. As always, experiment and modify. When you find the best methodology, you'll most likely also find that much less effort is necessary to make the rig sound great. Grab a few stagehands and let's go!

10/13/96 Julio Iglesias

Being a great sound engineer has many different aspects to it. One that is crucially important, yet often overlooked, is the art of stacking or flying your PA to give the most even coverage possible. As far as I'm concerned, this is one of the main criteria to be considered when choosing a PA, and definitely the main objective to be considered when placing the speakers on the stage or in the air.

Choosing the position of each speaker in the array is also important. Some manufacturers will suggest a certain way to pattern your speakers in the array to best suit different situations. I suggest that you start with what the manufacturer specifies and then eventually vary here and there to see if something different works better with your mixing style or the band's type of music and audience.

One pattern that has proven itself again and again to me is to fly or stack the speakers that you intend to throw the farthest (to the back, highest seats in the venue) at the top and inside (onstage) of your array. You will want a full-bandwidth speaker combo—whether that includes a long throw high-mid box and a long throw upper bass box or just a single full range cabinet—to take care of this long-throw situation. This becomes the main portion of your PA's EQ structure, and setting this to sound right at the back of the room is the first priority.

From there you will find that the speakers you use to cover the seats closer to the stage (in front and around the sides) will not have to work as hard in the low and low-mid area because that is being handled higher up in the PA. This may sound hard to swallow, but you really need to try it and see. If you are playing a venue such as an arena, amphitheater, or theatre, concentrate on getting the PA chunky and crisp at the farthest seats before you worry about what is happening at the mix position or closer to the stage. It may take a few trips up into the balcony or the back of the arena, but once you have assured yourself that the long-throw part of the PA is getting to the back, you can then fill in the rest of the room.

You will notice that you will now only need to add in the higher frequencies with the nearer portion of speakers because the low and low-mid frequencies in the long throw speakers are quite omni-directional, and will easily be enough for most of the room. If you only listen to the nearer set of speakers by themselves you will probably find that they are very thin and bright sounding, but try to forget what the individual bits of the PA are doing and think of the end result. The speakers around the side will most likely only need upper frequencies as well, to add to what the main speakers are doing. Now, by saying all of this I am assuming that you are using a multi-zone PA and have level and EQ control over all these zones. This isn't always the case with a budget show, but you can use the same concept by EQ'ing the upper boxes in your stack to sound right at the back of the hall and then adding in only what is needed (with amp level control) for the speakers nearer to the stage.

For anyone who has chased around low and low-mid clutter in PA systems and has just not been able to figure out where it's coming from, this will help incredibly. The main agenda is usually EQ'ing for front of house first and then trying to get the back of the hall bright enough. This is a little like chasing your tail, because as you brighten up the long throw, the front of house will now get increasingly bright and you almost have to start over. Take care of the long stuff first and then add in what's missing up close, which is usually only low level, higher frequency fill.

This has only been a recent revelation to me and has helped to clean up my mixes in the entire room a great deal. Part of the deal is to try to get very narrow pattern speakers to take care of the long-throw stuff and then as you get closer and closer to the stage, the speaker should have a wider and wider pattern. This may not be everyone's theory, but I can only vouch for what has worked for me. Make it great at the top and you won't have to do much at the bottom.

4/12/95 Van Halen

When you stack your PA speakers, you must always be aware of the direction they are pointing. Using the example of a small club system that might consist of three or four sub-bass speakers, a pair of midrange speakers, and two high-end horns per side, the coverage of sound is very critically dependent on where you have things pointing. This is especially true as frequency increases, which means that the high-end horns are going to be much more directional than the theoretically omni-directional low end.

Now we're dabbling in theory and these memos are supposed to be more about practical application, so let's look at common sense and trial and error. If you intend to cover a certain area of seats in a club with a full-frequency blend of sound and you find there is too much high end in one area and not enough in another, moving your high-end horns around a little is the first place to start. Most of the time this is all that is needed to shape the high-end coverage of a room. Where things get a little confusing is with sub-bass because in theory (there's that word again) this area of frequencies is much less directional than higher frequencies.

Anyone who has done sound for a while will tell you that sub-bass frequencies are more omni-directional than higher frequencies. This means that if you point a sub-bass speaker box in a particular direction, it will be very close to the same level at the side and only a little quieter behind the speaker; a horn-style high-end speaker box, on the other hand, is much louder in front than behind. The reason for saying all of this is that many engineers take this theory a little too much as pure fact and believe that it doesn't matter where you point your sub-bass speaker cabinets. They believe the sub coverage will be even because the sound comes out in an omni-directional pattern.

This is not always true, and I have had great success with various-sized PA systems getting even coverage in the lower frequencies by "shaping" the room, by means of differing the way the sub-bass speaker boxes are stacked. If you have a small club PA that consists of two bass speakers per side there isn't much you can do, but if you have more than three or four, this little bit of info is quite useful. Certain laws of physics lend a hand in deciding how bass reacts once it comes out of the speaker box and starts bouncing around. One trait that I'm sure everyone has experienced is the way bass tends to be thicker and boomier in the middle of the room than on the sides. This happens almost all the time.

What I have done in the past is to try to move the bass coverage pattern around by stacking more bass cabinets on the outside of the stack than towards the center. This seems to give a bit of a buildup on the sides of the room and pulls it away from the center. It is commonly known that if bass speakers are stacked to form one big speaker mouth, a phenomenon known as coupling occurs, and you seem to get more overall bass level from your sound system. In an effort to achieve this, many people stack sub-bass boxes in one big pile. What often follows is an accumulation of lows in one area of the room and less in other areas.

You may get a little less overall bass level at the mix position by moving bass bins to the outside of your stack, but an even mix everywhere in the room is a far greater reward than uneven thump as far as I'm concerned. For years it seemed that uneven coverage in venues was acceptable, mostly because the sound systems were much less intricate than they are nowadays, but in the present audio generation, every paying customer wants great sound. This is the best reason of all to attempt to steer the sub energy to the outsides of the venue as well as front of house. Don't be a sub-hog. Share the wealth by changing your sub-bass speaker placement.

CHAPTER 7

Working with the Audio Team

We're all in this together. Although the guys mixing the show tend to get most of the glory, the entire team is necessary to make it all happen. Large tours that play mainly in arenas usually have sound crews of roughly five or six guys. There can be a front-of-house mixer, a monitor mixer, system tech, monitor tech and two PA techs, or any combination of the above.

Anyone who manages personnel of any number knows even six guys (or gals) are enough for personal conflicts and character clashes. Most of us have been doing this long enough to have our own methodology and style which shows in everything we do, from miking up the stage to flying a sound system. When we work with a team of folks, we often have to meld our collective minds and techniques to produce smooth flowing procedures for getting things done.

The system tech often ends up being the sound crew chief, as he tends to be there from the planning stage on up. He or she may actually handpick the entire crew aside from the mixers, or the mixers may actually have a choice in choosing the team. As a mixer I can honestly say that there are certain folks I insist on having on every tour if I have any say in the matter. (Fumi, you know who I 'm talking about). It's a comfort thing, a feeling of security knowing the PA is going to get up in the air as soon as possible with all the components patched correctly and positioned where you want them. This allows you the most time in the day to tune the system and fiddle with all those knobs. You can't do much with it if it's on the ground.

It's your responsibility, no matter what your job is, to find a place in the crew and fulfill your job description every day. Everyone will be counting on you to be "there" in whatever capacity that might be. That also includes attitude and effort. It's a big job getting an entire rig and stage patched every day so we all have to work hard and work together. Smiles and positive vibes are greatly appreciated. Doing multiple back-to-back nights can drain us all, and it's hard to be a "Hallmark Greeting Card" every day, but do what you can to help the team have a bit of fun in the process. Respect the people you're working with and soon you'll be the guy everyone asks for each time they head out on tour.

And remember, engineers who treat their crew as vital links in the chain and commend their hard work tend to start "knob-twisting" earlier than the grumpy bear who strolls off the bus at the crack of noon, wondering why his latte isn't waiting for him along with his keys to the rig.

"SO HAPPY TOGETHER"

6/17/95 Van Halen

A sound team working for an artist or band must work together. This may seem like a given, but there are a lot of people in the music business who look right past the needs of others to make sure their own world is safe and cozy.

I don't mean this in a harsh way, because in the end if you screw up your gig you're sure to hear about it from the top. I merely want to state the importance of an entire sound crew working together. This applies to a small team of just a front-of-house and monitor mixer as well as a stadium touring sound crew of eight or more. Everyone needs to be clear and respectful of the other teammates' procedures and routines to make the whole day and tour go smoother. When I begin working with a new sound crew, I'll usually sit down and let them know how I like to have the day go, or at least have this discussion with my sound crew chief.

Without trying to be the one who orchestrates the proceedings, I try to get everyone's views on how, as a team, things can be done in the smoothest manner. This starts with the load-in and carries on through to line check, soundcheck, and the show. Everyone knowing their jobs is a vital concern, and by that I mean two things: Firstly, everyone should be skilled enough to perform the job they have been hired to do, and secondly, everyone should be clear as to what is being asked of them on a day-to-day basis.

If the PA setup is unorganized and the speakers aren't even stacked or flown, and the monitor guy has his power and console hooked up and is ready to go while everyone else is trying to work through the noise, tensions are going to rise. The setup and line check/soundcheck proceedings should be relatively the same day in and day out.

Whose system will be tuned first should be decided by majority vote. A monitor guy can't EQ wedges while music is blasting through the PA, and a front-of-house guy can't work on drum sounds while the monitor guy is getting the bass guitar level in the monitors on stage. Work on getting a routine going.

On one tour, we did things kind of like this: After everything was set up and the power was metered and checked, we would turn on all the consoles and amplifiers, and both the monitor guy and myself would run pink noise through our speakers. Once this was done, he would take off to eat lunch while I would spend about 20 minutes or more tuning the PA. When I was finished I would go to lunch while he EQ'd the monitor system, and when he was all through we would line check the instruments on stage. Our procedure for this was to check each input on stage at the same time, and not move on until it was acceptable in both mixing boards. After the line check was done, he would take about 20 minutes on stage to get the instruments soundchecked in the monitors and then I would check them in the house.

The main reason this routine worked as well as it did was our decision to have things flow the same way every day. With this agreement in place, we were never left standing around being impatient, waiting for the other to finish. Work together with your sound partners and find a plan that makes your day flow more smoothly. It will make for better friendships and better engineering.

7/10/97 Ted Nugent

How many of you out there have had the frustration of doing a show with a local sound company, or an installed system, and the tech in charge is not sure—or completely doesn't know—which amplifier channels control certain components in specific speaker boxes? This really becomes a problem when you need to turn down a certain bank of components, such as the high end in a group of speakers. Many times, especially when you have to ground stack your PA, the high end will be a little too much down front and you will need to turn down the horns on just the bottom row of speakers.

If the representative from the sound company or installed club/theatre PA isn't sure which amp channels go to which speaker box, you can spend many frustrating minutes searching for the right channel that will do what you want. At this point a haunting feeling comes over you, wondering if he has turned down other high-end components on some boxes that might be pointing in a direction where you are definitely needing high end.

This is not always the easiest thing to tell if the PA is flown, as you can't get in front of the speakers to confirm if the right adjustment is being made. The thing to do is have the sound company rep run through the various amplifier channels before you ever start listening to music or EQ'ing things. Get him to explain to you how he has the PA divided up (amp channel wise) and then try to follow along as he runs up the various amp volumes, and see if things seem to be separated as he said.

If the tech is not sure, nicely suggest that they run up one amp channel at a time and then document which bank of speaker components it is driving. If you can pleasantly suggest labeling the various amp channels as he goes, you have won the lottery. This will make you feel so much more confident that the things being turned down are affecting the right speaker boxes and *only* those speaker boxes. This should not turn into a situation where the sound company tech takes offense, or says that he knows his system thoroughly and gets indignant.

If there is time in the day to go through this little drill, it is simply a way for you, as the guest mixer, to feel most comfortable with an unfamiliar system. The sound company or PA rep should take pride in making the sound engineer mixing on his system feel like everything is under control, and no mistakes are going to occur that could undermine the work he is trying to do. Situations have occurred for me where things seemed fine even as I fired up the system at tuning time, and so I left some of these questions unanswered. However, at show time (or while the opening act was playing their set), I would feel the need to adjust the level of a certain group of speakers. Upon asking the sound rep to make those adjustments, a foggy look would come over his face, followed by a look towards the heavens to try to visually trace which speaker cable is going to which speaker. This does not help all concerned to feel certain that the right speaker/amp level adjustments will be made. Sometimes at this point it is better to leave things as they are if your PA rep is not completely sure. Remember next time to insist that your tech for the day is confident in his system, so you can be confident with your mix.

"CHASING YOUR TAIL"

9/16/95 Van Halen

Troubleshooting is an acquired art form. I've known some sound techs that couldn't mix to save their lives, and prefer not to. Their passion is sound tech work and some of these guys are the best troubleshooters around. This book concerns itself with mixing, so I'll leave the advanced audio troubleshooting lessons for another place and time, but I would like to discuss obtaining a basic knowledge to get to the root of a problem quickly when it involves mixing.

One thing that happens a lot on the road is finding an input that is not working during line check, or sometimes during a show. There is a simple, basic system to follow that will help determine the source of the problem quickly and accurately. I like to start with the microphone first. This is the place where the sound originates and a likely place to start looking for a problem. One thing you want to note at this point is whether the mic that is causing you problems is a condenser mic (requiring 48V phantom power) or a dynamic mic (requires no external power). If the mic that has gone down is a condenser mic, I would suggest you first try putting another condenser mic on the same mic cable to see if you now have signal. If you do, then you have obviously found the problem to be a bad microphone.

If you find that there is still no signal, I would then suggest you try putting a dynamic mic like a Shure SM57 on the mic line to see if the problem lies in the transfer of phantom power to the microphone. If you find that you are now hearing the mic, you can assume that you have a 48V phantom power problem. I would then search the variables that allow 48V power to get to the microphone. Confirm that the phantom power is turned on for that channel and check to see if your XLR pin 1 connection on your microphone cable and snake line is intact all the way down the pipe.

If neither mic gives you any signal, you must carry on. I like to follow the path that carries the signal from the mic to the mixing boards. The mic cable is the next obvious choice, followed by the subsnake box on stage and then the splitter box that splits signal to the monitor and front-of-house board. After that you are pretty much left with checking the snake and channel inputs on your consoles to see if they might be the problem.

Be sure to check things in some kind of order and develop a system that is your own. Repeat it every time you hunt down a problem and be sure not to jump a step or two in your order, as you then have to backtrack to some middle ground and try to remember if you checked there or not. A good rule of thumb as well is to have both the front-of-house and monitor engineers listening in as you go along to make sure that the problem isn't just at one end of a snake. If the monitor guy has signal and you don't out front, then the problem lies between the stage split and your console. Be thorough and repeatable and you won't end up chasing your tail in the process of locating a problem.

CHAPTER 8

Managing Your Time

At least once a day the comment spews forth from a casual observer: "How many days did it take you folks to put all this equipment in here?"

"Well," you nonchalantly reply, "we started at 8 a.m. this morning." That usually achieves the jaw-dropping stare of a person experiencing their first UFO sighting. It is a little hard to believe, isn't it? It happens only because a combination of tons of experience, a great plan and superb gear preparation in the production build happened first.

But what happens when the day isn't unfolding quite the way you planned? Does this innocent question conjure up nightmarish flashbacks of gigs gone horribly wrong? It does for me. Eavesdropping on the production manager's conversation with the lead truck driver and hearing comments like, "The rigging truck is WHERE?" will usually be an indication of the kind of day you have before you. In the end, the show must go on, and it will. It simply means you will have to do four hours of work in two, and it may mean the show's a little late. It has happened before, so don't sweat it. The worst thing is when the trucks finally arrive and you aren't ready. Or, you get your gear finally, and disorganization on your part causes your piece of the pie to hold up the show.

All you can do is produce the most concentrated amount of work in the time slot you're given. Objectives you might have attended to after the PA is in the air might be accomplished while it's being flown, and console continuity checks might be conducted as soon as your front-of-house package is patched. But, as you'll read in "Don't put the cart before the horse," this personal timesaving soundcheck procedure also has its limitations, as some things should be in place before you move forward. So, read on; time is money.

"DON'T PUT THE CART BEFORE THE HORSE"

8/12/97 Ted Nugent

How many times have you experienced "hurry up and wait" mode as the day rushes past much quicker than you would hope? The schedule calls for a 4 p.m. soundcheck, and at 3 p.m. you're just getting the last of the speakers plugged in and the PA fired up. It's tough for everybody concerned to get enough time to do his or her thing in a thorough way when this happens. The best plan is for everyone to realize that time is short and that the quickest test of the equipment is what's needed. This goes for front-of-house and monitor engineers as well as band roadies. If everyone does a condensed version of their normal routine, all can be done to satisfaction.

The secret is to try to let some basic things happen before you go ahead and listen to instruments in the sound system. You must try to allocate at least five minutes or so to tune the PA and get some of the bad frequencies out, and then let the monitor guy have a quick ring out on stage. I think it's important to let the drum tech get the drums tuned to his liking, because if you rush him into a premature soundcheck and he hasn't tuned all of his toms, he may just go ahead and retune them after soundcheck, and it kind of defeats the purpose of checking them in the first place. I agree it's important to get a line check done so that you know all of the mics and lines are working on stage and at the monitors, but let the instrument techs on stage get things somewhat dialed in before you listen in the PA. This ensures that you will get the real deal come soundcheck time. Some times we have no choice but to rush. Whenever possible, plan the rush to work out best in the end for all involved. The good thing is, rush hour will never bother you nearly as much in the future.

Extreme European Tour '94

Date: Sept. 12th
City: Madrid, Spain
Venue: Las Ventas

1st Call: Riggers, Lights, Stage Mgr.
Lobby Call: 6:45 am
Venue Call: 7:00 am

2nd Call: Rest of lighting crew, Audio crew chief
Lobby Call: 7:45 am
Venue Call: 8:00 am

3rd Call: Rest of Audio crew
Lobby Call: 8:45 am
Venue Call: 9:00 am

4th Call: Mixers, Backline
Lobby Call: 9:45 am
Venue Call: 10:00 am

Breakfast: 7:00 am
Lunch: 12:00 pm
Dinner: 5:00 pm

Sound Check: 4:30 pm
Doors: 6:00 pm
Opening Act: 7:30 pm
Extreme: 9:00
Curfew: 11:00

Check out of Hotel? Yes
Travel: After show bus to Barcelona

This example of a tour call-time sheet gives a basic breakdown of when crew members leave the hotel or get out of their bunks. A well-orchestrated load-in involves dumping trucks in an intelligent, logical order and crew call times reflect that logical order. When things go wrong, it's best to abandon the orchestration and rely on the logical.

"TIME IS ON YOUR SIDE"

8/9/97 Ted Nugent

It has happened to almost all of us. If it hasn't, consider yourself one of the blessed. The PA you booked for the show is late, or the lighting company still has the lights on the stage at 2 p.m. and your show is at 7:30 p.m. Whenever you're pressed for time and you have a whole new console and processing to get dialed in, use your time wisely.

As soon as the power is up to front of house, I like to make sure that my entire drive chain (e.g. console, EQ, crossover, power, and speakers) is functioning, and then give the monitor team a chance to check all their mixes. When you're both sure all your gear works, tune the PA as quickly as possible and then let the monitor guy get to it, or vice-versa. Now's your chance to make up time. While he's testing, set compressor levels and gain on vocals. While they're getting drum sounds onstage, set gates and check effects. You can do all of this in headphones and not disturb them, and then when your turn comes you're way more ahead of the game.

You will find a pattern for this that works best, especially if you are doing a lot of one-offs on a different console and PA every day. And you will undoubtedly find other shortcuts and time-saving practices in your routine. You will also discover where you wasted time in the day and paid the price later. Use the quiet time to your advantage, and be sure to get a bite to eat, as I have learned that missing dinner seldom means a better show.

PART FOUR: TUNING THE PA

TUNING THE PA

After all the planning, building, setting up and powering up are done, it's time to make this thing sound like something we would like to listen to. This is often the time of the day when the local crew and your audio crew go for lunch. You're often left with an empty room and a monstrous "boom box." You're on your own.

Fear not, young engineer, you are not the first to have traveled this road. Equipped with enough technology to make your head spin (or bleed) and blessed with golden ears trained and developed over years of club mixing, you are finally left at the crossroads of audio destiny. The giant sound system has met the giant room. Let me take your hand and give you a map with some landmarks to provide you safe passage through this reverberant jungle.

It's a two-fold process consisting of EQ and delay. You can't successfully EQ without first aligning your PA. We came close for years but it's a new world, and that world has better ears and multimedia than it used to. We have to keep up, and technology is available to help us do just that. You can grab all the manuals that are available, have your audio guru walk you through the steps, read helpful insights like the ones to follow, but the optimum results will come after trial and error. Don't be afraid to make a mistake. Grab a slider or a knob and go "twistin' by the pool." Remember that the manufacturers of your speaker boxes have spent long hours attempting to make their product sound as good as it can "out of the box," so don't necessarily start hacking and chewing away at the graph right away. However, they can't know how many you are going to throw up in the air or how the room you're mixing in will respond, so you will have to make adjustments to their fine product's response sooner or later.

Whether you use a form of analysis tool, your God-given listening devices, or a combination of the two (highly recommended), remember that the foundation is always the key to a strong finished product. Build the system correctly and fly it correctly. Allow yourself multiple adjustment points (delay and EQ) in each zone and then the rest is up to you.

Be artistic, be technical, and be creative. Grab a knob and let 'er rip.

CHAPTER 9

EQ

Everyone's a critic and everyone's a sound engineer. These are two basic facts of life. We all have our own ideas regarding a correctly tuned sound system, or at least the sound that's pleasing to us. I say this because in the end it's going to be up to you. Don't doubt your natural "EQ curve." Everyone may not necessarily agree with what you like, but they weren't hired to mix the band. You were.

The counterpoint to this is basics and fundamentals. If you throw five different styles of music into your car's CD player, they will all have some basic foundation of tonal balance. If you decide to blaze the trail of "alternative tonal choices," you may find yourself explaining that theory to the folks with the bleeding eardrums in row 5. Conclusion: there are limitations to where you can go with this.

Understand your gear and listen to others mix. You'll get an idea of what you like and don't like. In the end, you can't go very wrong making the PA sound like the CD the artist just released. At least it's a starting point.

"EQ THE DUDES TOO"

7/6/95 Van Halen

I've always believed that there is no "right" mix or "perfect" sound, because we all perceive things a little differently. Your own version of what sounds good may be completely different from someone else's. Because of this I think that all of us who call ourselves sound engineers have a slightly different method of tuning and adjusting the equalization of our PAs.

I like to use pink noise to make sure all of the various frequency bands (lows, mids, and highs) are even for the left and right side of the PA. Then I run some pink noise through the subs and lows to see what the response of the room is like when I boost some low frequencies. After that I blast the room with a quick shot of full frequency pink noise to see what the reverb time of the room is. At this point I'm ready to listen to some program music on a DAT. I always use the same song or two so that I can relate what I'm hearing today to what my standard reference is. This is my method and I'm not saying it's right, or the only way, but it has worked for me. One of the problems that can occur from using program music is if that song has certain particular frequencies that are predominate. This can give you a false reading of the PA system and room's frequency response.

You will usually learn what to look out for after using that song for a while, but what I suggest doing is "test EQ'ing" (by boosting or cutting frequencies to see what effect they have) while the band is running through some songs during soundcheck. You may sometimes have to explain yourself to the band as they may think something weird is going on (if they're not in their plastic bubbles called "in-ear monitors") as you're boosting low end momentarily in the house, but I think it is well worth the explaining. You can mold and shape the curve of your equalizers to fit the band's frequency response in that room, that day. It's also very useful for finding out what frequencies are harsh and biting on the top end. Try to do it quickly with quick bursts of boost and cut. While DAT tapes and pink noise are helpful for getting you close, the band you are mixing that night is going to determine how the PA should be tuned.

"SMOOTH OFF THE EDGES"

7/19/94 Ted Nugent

High-end "edginess" does not always show itself when a PA is quiet. As you turn things up the highs will tend to increase, and not always proportionally. When you tune the PA with your voice and/or music this must always be kept in mind. A lot depends on the type of act or program that will be mixed during the performance. If the average volume of the show tends to be quiet, turning the PA up real loud to tune will tend to give you an over-EQ'd and dull system at show time. If you are mixing a rock show or something of considerable level, tuning the system at a nice quiet volume may cause problems later when you fire things up and the level jumps sky high. You will most likely find yourself peeling paint off the walls with high end, and this to me is one of the most annoying things to hear at a rock show, or any show.

But blasting everyone with a kickin' CD is not always the most popular thing to do during the day while the rest of the road crew is trying to set up equipment. This is just something that everyone will have to give you a break on, and I suppose the trick is to limit the amount of time that you turn things up good and loud. It is extremely important, however, to smooth out the hot spots in the high-end area of the sound system by tuning at a level that is consistent with show volume.

This also goes for tuning with your voice. If the singer tends to give a good yell every now and then, you should do this as well and see how the PA responds when you hit the mic with some bright high-endy vocal. While you have things cooking at high level during the tuning and EQ'ing process, try to do a quick walk around to see how the various zones of PA are fitting into the big picture. Often times, at low level, you will think the Front Fill speakers are not loud or bright enough and you will give them a nudge up in level. Then, when the show starts, these speakers (which you can't always hear from the mix position) are killing the people up front. Get things smooth and the coverage even and consistent during the afternoon and take the complaints from the lighting guys then, instead of the complaints from the paying customers later.

"I'VE LOST IT, NOW HOW CAN I GET IT BACK?"

6/22/93 Van Halen

Everything you do while trying to make one part of your mix perfect will always seem to affect another part. If you turn one thing up it naturally makes another thing sound quieter. If you brighten something up it tends to make other things sound dull. All things that you do must work for the common good of the end result: your best mix. This fact is never more evident than with EQ. The cuts and boosts that you do to your main system EQ will determine how every one of your channel EQs will look. If you can get the speaker components relatively even in level before reaching for the system EQ, you'll be off to a good start. Hopefully your system curve will be displayed on a real time analyzer as a smooth response with a gentle, even roll-off as you get to the higher frequencies. With a "flat" system to start with, all channel EQ has a solid base, and it should be just a little boost or cut from there.

As you start to dig away at your main system EQ, you will have to make up those lost frequencies on certain instruments with channel EQ. This is so often done with drum channels. The PA may seem overly bright when you tune it with a song or pink noise, so you start taking out high end from your graphic or parametric EQ. Pretty soon you think you have things pretty much smoothed out and you start checking drum sounds. The drummer/tech starts hitting the kick drum and it needs a little high end to cut through. Then the snare sounds kind of clunky and needs some crack so you add a little high end. Then you check the cymbals and they could use some real high stuff to sweeten them up... and on and on you go. The thing you should notice is that you had to add that high-end channel EQ to the drums because you lost it all from your system EQ.

Now, I don't suggest killing everyone with high end on the guitars and vocals just so you don't have to add EQ on your drums, but compromises have to be made. Every time you boost or cut bunches of EQ, you run into the problem of phase coloration affecting your sound.

What does that mean to you and me? Lots of EQ is electronically not the smartest thing to do and you will notice things sounding weird. How do you get around this problem? The first and best solution is to start with a flat EQ'd sound system and then try to pick the right microphones for each instrument. If the mic you're presently using is not giving an accurate representation of the original sound out in the house, then find a mic that does. If everything sounds great but you have one guitar amp that sounds all scratchy and filled with high end, then try to fix this one problem by having the guitar player adjust his sound or by picking a different mic. Sometimes, simply trying different mic positions with the mic you're using is all you need. If you don't have the time or resources to pick the perfect mics, the answer is compromise. Take out a little high end from your graphic and your guitars and then boost a little on your drums. The key word here is little. The less you cut and boost the better you'll be in the long run. Don't get caught looking for your mix in the lost and found.

"LET'S GO FOR A STROLL"

3/12/95 Van Halen

I'm a firm believer that being prepared well before show time is the best way to avoid looking like a fool during the show. If you didn't check the bass guitar during your soundcheck and then, as the show is about to begin, you turn on the bass and the direct box is buzzing like a Homelite, you only have yourself to blame. This is why I have a consistent checklist of line check and soundcheck procedures that I follow every day to ensure I don't forget anything.

One thing I do with the monitor engineer after all the lines have been checked and the backline technicians have safely returned to the bus is check the vocal mic through the PA. I usually check the microphone from out front with my own voice to suss out the hot spots of the room that day, but after it's in the ballpark, it's good to get together with the monitor engineer and listen to the combined effect of the monitors and house together. I like to start by listening to the mic with the monitor guy talking through it with only the stage monitors turned on. This will give me an idea of the frequencies coming off the stage that may interfere or couple up with the PA once I'm turned on out front. If you've got a monitor guy who's willing to work with you, he'll help you out by pulling a few of the prominent low or low-mid frequencies out from the monitors to help when everything is on together. Usually, once the PA is on, any low-end stuff that might appear to be missing from the monitors will seem to come back and the monitor engineer will be happy again. Once we're happy with the stage sound I will go about trying to find my loudest level in the PA before feedback.

I like to start with the vocal mic downstage center if the singer is in a fixed position, with the mic on a stand. Even if she is mobile, she will usually spend most of her time there. If the main vocal mic is in a fixed position elsewhere on the stage, see what your maximum level is with the mic in that position. From there I will have the monitor engineer walk around the stage to see if there are any feedback hot spots. The majority of the problems happen as they approach the ground-stacked PA at the downstage left and right corners of the stage. It is at this same downstage corner area that you will find the singer getting dangerously close to being right under a flown PA as well. Have the monitor engineer walk down to these areas and see at what level on the fader the microphone starts to give you feedback trouble.

Sometimes the feedback may only be at one particular frequency and you can locate it one your channel EQ and have it ready to pull out if the singer goes to that area. Knowing the exact frequencies where the trouble will be saves you from having to search or guess during the show.

Daytime Checklist:

- Make sure AC power is metered and acceptable (118V to 123V are good boundaries, with less than 3V between ground and neutral).
- Check that all your gear powers up and settles in correctly. If any warning lights come up now is the time to shut things off again. When you are doing a show outside look closely for displays and power ON lights as they are not always easy to see in the sunlight.
- When you have a moment, check that crucial knobs have not been spun or switches like input gain pads have not been pushed in or out. Give entire gear inventory a quick look for abnormalities.
- Turn pink noise or test tone on at the console and run signal through various signal chains. Check all components of the chain (Group out, Master out, eq, X-over, compressors) for signal lights and continuity.
- When able, run pink noise (or source, e.g. music) through each signal chain. (An example would be running noise through the left-main PA speaker chain) You want to check each component in that speaker cluster, lows, mids, and highs for example, and then move on to the next speaker cluster.
- When you know all components are working, A/B the like components left and right. (E.g. main highs left/right). When all speakers check out for equal level and tonality, you can move on to delay-time finding (if you are set up for this).
- Find delay times for all zones (if applicable).
- Check for general hums and buzzes if you haven't in the last couple steps.
- Get audio crew together for line check. Always check each instrument with everyone listening to avoid erroneous detection of problems.
- Tune the PA now or before line check. This process usually changes from day to day.
- When your turn comes, listen to each instrument and vocal and check inserts (gates, compressors) for continuity and function if you didn't have time to check them during line check.
- You're ready for the band!

A step-by-step checklist to get you going every day. You may not follow things exactly in this order but this is a rough guide that works for me. The important lesson is to develop your own checklist and be true to each step day after day.

"MASTER THE ART OF EQ'ING"

4/19/96 Julio Iglesias

This memo relates to the previous one in that it discusses the use of multiple zones of PA. The focus of this discussion is where to direct your attention once the show has begun. During the day, as you go along EQ'ing each of the different clusters of PA, you will undoubtedly decide on a curve for each zone that you are happy with. After the zones are combined and you play some music or listen to the band at soundcheck, you may decide to touch up the sound of one or more of the zones individually. The soundcheck is the time to do this.

Walk around as the band is playing and get a fix on the EQ you want in each of the zones. If you find the front fills are too bright, then immediately deal with it. Once the show starts, the only way to know what is going on in the various areas of the room is to reference it to what you heard earlier. You can also send an assistant out strolling and trust him to tell you which EQ to alter. The point is that you can't really know what is happening in areas that you are not hearing.

For this reason, I suggest an overall EQ that might be inserted on the master outputs of the board, or may come before the other zone EQs in the EQ chain. Leave this master EQ flat during the day and EQ the zones of PA as they need with their own separate EQ. Then, when the show starts, you can simply go to the master EQ and notch or boost the frequency curve for the system as a whole, and not have to go into each zone's EQ and change it individually. This may seem a little bit too simple and not exact enough, but the point is that during the day you made each zone to sound about right, and if something is not quite right when the show starts it probably needs adjusting just about everywhere. You can send your assistant into the various zones for a listen, and he may advise you not to change a certain EQ setting in one particular zone, but generally, if something is sticking out of the frequency balance as the show starts, changing it throughout the room will help to make the change more effective.

One exception to this is when a high frequency is feeding back from the lead singer's mic. It might be helpful if you take a little of that frequency out only in the speakers that are close to the mic, like front fills and speakers pointing to the front and center of the room). You might not want to take those high frequencies out of long throw speakers that might need all the highs you can give them. This suggestion might not work for everyone, but it does help to make each EQ move simpler and more overly influential in the heat of the battle. Put the master EQ at the top of the order to speed (and hopefully help) things along.

11/4/96 Julio Iglesias

When you're tuning a new system that has various zones of speakers, it is important to keep track of what you're listening to. If you fire up the whole PA at once and begin playing music through it, or tuning with your voice, you may unknowingly be chasing your tail if you find some frequencies are bothering you and they just won't seem to go away. The problem may be that you're EQ'ing those frequencies out of one zone and they may actually be coming from another group of speakers that you're not getting to with the main system EQ.

There are a couple of ways to tackle this, but one important thing is to get the different zones of PA balanced in regards to level before you begin the task of EQ'ing. Here is what I would suggest after running some pink noise through the speakers to test their working status. Run some noise again, or speak into a mic. Turn on all the different zones of PA (long throw, main array, side array, down fill, and front fill) and have a walk around. See if the general level of all the zones is in balance. If the down fill speakers are killing you when you get down front, then pull the level down on these and then continue. Get the level on the front fills to blend evenly into the overhead flown PA so it is as seamless as possible.

After this is accomplished, you can begin EQ'ing. I would suggest you start out with one zone at a time, beginning with the long throw speakers and working down the flown array from there. When you do the long throw, down fill and front fill zones (those which are not facing the mix console) it may take some walking around to be sure the EQ choices you've made at the board are right when you get into their throw pattern. The main point to remember is that level very much affects EQ. If you are trying to EQ the main speakers and the side speakers are really loud and bouncing off empty seats, you will find yourself trying to get rid of things in the main system's EQ that are really problems in another zone. Once you've made each zone sound decent, add them all together and see where you are.

Remember that front fill and down fill speakers don't always need to sound full on their own, because once they combine with big clusters of speakers they might only be used to throw some high end into a dull area. Remember also to get your zones level before you reach for the EQ sliders. A well-balanced system will often lead to a well-balanced checkbook.

"IF LIFE IMITATES ART, LET YOUR TUNING MUSIC IMITATE THE ARTIST"

5/14/96 Julio Iglesias

As sound engineers, we should be very aware of what we use as a reference to correctly tune a sound system. Some people will just use pink noise and a real-time analyzer to tune, and others will be more confident in listening to the sound of their own voices through a particular microphone. Others like to listen to music, something they know very well or something that seems to work particularly well in balancing the PA. I personally like to use a combination of all three, but I pay close attention to the type of music I'm using when working with various artists. I believe the most important aspect of the track or tracks of music you are using is that you are very familiar with it.

Listen to the song a lot on headphones or on a good sounding home or car stereo to really know what that song sounds like in an acoustically pleasant environment. When you then play that song through a PA system you should be able to discern if the system is out of balance frequency-wise or if the room is causing things to sound different. The next issue is what kind of music to play for various styles of music you might be mixing. If you have only ever used one song for your entire career and you know exactly what that song should sound like when played through a sound system, I would stick with what you know—even if it's Steely Dan and the rest of the crew wants to kill you—but I would strongly suggest that you try various styles of tuning songs for a couple of reasons.

For starters, if you have been using a Metallica song for years and you are asked to mix a Julio Iglesias show, you will probably get about 15 seconds into the track before someone will kindly (or not so kindly) ask you to shut it off. It can be very annoying to the people around you, and to properly tune a PA you need at least a few minutes—a few minutes that shouldn't be complete agony for everyone else in the building. Conversely, if you are mixing Metallica, you may get similar responses to a Julio Iglesias tuning song. The point is, if the people you are working with enjoy the song, they will tend to let you tune a little longer, and you can probably get things more in the ballpark. Secondly, various styles of music and artists require various styles of PA tuning.

A tuning song that accurately represents the style of music you will be mixing that evening will probably get you closer to your desired starting point. I have about four songs that I rotate depending on who it is that I'm working for. One other thing to remember is to tune, at least for a little while, at the approximate show volume. If show level is quite loud you won't want to do this for too long, but give yourself an idea of how things will be at that level. The frequency response of the song you choose, at the level the band plays, should imitate the actual sound of the band you will be mixing.

"LEVELHEADED"

9/6/94 Jon Secada

This memo goes hand in hand with another one called "Master the art of EQ'ing, page 82." In that discussion I noted the value of putting a master EQ ahead of all of your zone EQs. This is so that you could reach for trouble frequencies during the show and keep your entire zone EQ consistent, without having to go for five or six EQs. What we will look into here concerns level more than EQ, although we all know that the two things go hand in hand much of the time.

Following the basic premise of the master EQ theory in the other memo, we want to keep in mind that there are a few exceptions, one being a radical level change from soundcheck or tuning time to show time. This can occur if you tune at a very quiet level and then adjust your various zone EQs around this level. As is discussed in the previous memo, try to tune or at least have a final listen to the various zones at a volume that somewhat resembles show level. If you tune too quietly and then the band doesn't come in for soundcheck, you may find that when the show starts you have to crank things up, and things can get very bright when this happens.

If this is the case, you must be careful about speakers that are very close to people's ears, like front fill and down fill speakers. Drastic level changes will hugely affect EQ curves, and near fill speakers that sounded nice and smooth during tuning may get dangerously bright and offensive when jacked way up. You may be able to hear this from 100 feet away but most likely you will not. The master EQ theory is great if you're making minor level and EQ changes but if the level change is dramatic, be sure to do individual EQ checks to the front fill speakers by sending someone into the front rows to listen.

The secret to not getting caught with this sudden change is to do a proper zone-to-zone EQ process during the day and then walk each of these zones with some music playing at show level boogie to be sure the EQ stays consistent and safe. My theory is that it's better to be a little bit dull and quiet with up-close speakers and hope that side fills and stage volume fill in what's missing than to blow people's heads off. Although it always annoys the people you are working with to check your PA's EQ with loud music, it really must be done for a short time if the band you are mixing wants the show to be loud. Definitely use the master EQ theory, but spend the time to get your individual zone EQ all the way right before show time, and keep levelheaded.

"CENTER OF ATTENTION"

3/10/96 Julio Iglesias

With most of the bands we mix, the lead vocal is the focal point of the show and often the artist that the people paid to see. This isn't always the case with rock bands, as the whole package is the focus of attention, but in general the lead vocal is going to be the loudest thing in the mix and the tuning of the PA should conform to the sound of the singer's voice.

Most sound engineers go through a similar routine every day to tune up the sound system. One of the steps in this process is speaking into a mic (I've suggested elsewhere to use the same mic as the lead vocalist uses) from the front-of-house mix position and removing unwanted frequencies in the PA. This should be dictated by the sound of the system in the room that day. Doing this will get you very close and give you a good idea of how the mic will sound at the console, but we don't always think about how the mic sounds in the PA from the viewpoint of standing on stage. The lead vocalist's perception of the sound of his voice in the sound system is taken from his position at center stage, not from the front of house. This perception has changed of late with the use of in-ear monitors, but getting the singer's feel from downstage center is important. Singers will sometimes say, after you have spent a good deal of time tuning their vocal mic from the front-of-house position, that their mic doesn't sound good to them on stage.

It is very easy at this point to shift the blame solely onto the shoulders of the monitor engineer and say that it sounds great in the house. This may very well be the truth, but the best way to absolutely know for sure how that mic sounds on stage is to go up there and find out. As you move up the ladder of success in this business you will be blessed to work with better and better equipment. And one of the treats of working on big tours is having a remote EQ control that you can take to the stage. After I tune the sound of my voice in the PA from front of house I will take my remote EQ controller and go to the stage to have a listen. I have the ability to mute various sections of the system and hear how the vocal sounds from stage in each one of these.

If you're not lucky enough to have this luxury, I would suggest having someone "drive" from front of house as you stand at center stage. Have them mute various sections of the PA and listen to each one independently. Call out the frequencies to be adjusted and have him make the moves for you. Often I will discover that one section of the PA has some undesirable frequencies that I wasn't hearing from out front, and by removing those frequencies in only that section, the sound of the vocal cleans up in the entire sound system. You may discover that one frequency, or a small band of frequencies, sounds larger on stage than from front of house. You might want to make an EQ change on the vocal channel EQ out front and sacrifice a little "meat" in the mix to make things work better overall when the monitors and main sound system combine.

The monitor guy should also be a part of the solution during this process and help by pulling out some overly large frequency humps if it helps the combined sound. The only way to know if the EQ'ing of the vocal mic is good everywhere is to stand in the shoes of the lead vocalist, or at least stand where the shoes of the lead vocalist will be, and have a listen for yourself. It's better for the vocalist to be the center of attention come show time, not you!

"GO A-STROLLIN'"

9/15/97 Engelbert Humperdinck

Be sure to take a stroll around the venue during soundcheck. When you are tuning the PA with music before the band arrives, you may think you have a good idea of how things sound in different areas of the room, but things usually sound quite different when the band is playing. During the show you are pretty much confined to the mixing board, so the only way to get a clear picture of the sound throughout the room is to walk around during soundcheck. It's a good idea to have an assistant that you trust walk around during the show and give you a general picture of how things are, but you'll always want to feel that you have been there before and you know what he's talking about. It's better to miss a cue during soundcheck, such as a guitar solo, than to have an unevenly balanced PA for an entire show.

If the singer is the star of the show, you often have a soundcheck with the band before the star arrives. This is the best opportunity to walk the room. And I do mean walk. Just because the balcony in that theater you're playing is three levels up with 20 stairs per level, don't wimp out and not make the trek. Every person buying a ticket deserves a fine mix, and as soon as I get off my soapbox I'm going to go walk the balcony of the room I'm mixing today, just to show you all up. Cruise the joint, and give everyone the fabulous mix you hear at the console.

5/9/96 Julio Iglesias

Part of the EQ'ing process should always include listening to your own voice through the main PA speakers. Listening to music can sometimes be a little deceiving in relation to how the vocal part of your mix will be, so it's a good idea to do a round of EQ'ing using the voice you know best—your own. The problem with EQ'ing to your own voice is that if you are the sound engineer for the band, chances are you probably won't be singing lead vocal for the band that night.

With this in mind, get a start on some general EQ with your voice and get the PA to a sound quality you can be happy with, but always keep in mind the tonal characteristics of the lead singer of the band. Your radio DJ voice may sound fantastic through the speakers, but if your singer is female and she shrieks like a banshee when she performs her vocal magic, you probably haven't steered the PA EQ in the right direction. I've never been one to sing into a mic to EQ, because frankly I can't sing a note and I don't have a mic in the shower at home, but you have to try to learn the tonal characteristics of the singer and mimic that general vocalizing with your own voice.

If the singer has a high- or mid-sounding voice with little or no bottom end and body, you will want to EQ by simulating this type of tone. You'll probably find that when you use a normal speaking voice it may sound very muddy and thick, but it will likely be just what that singer needs EQ-wise to fill out her voice. The same holds true for level. You don't want to yell into a mic and EQ for that if the singer is a whisperer. Another area where this applies is mic technique. If the singer sings with the mic six inches to a foot away from her mouth, speaking directly into the mic and EQ'ing that way will give you a very false EQ representation.

If it's the first time you are EQ'ing a certain PA I would suggest that you go about getting things close with your standard EQ practices and speak as you normally would into the mic to get the system sounding like your voice. After that is done you should then fine tune around the loudest microphone on the stage—the lead vocalist's mic. One last note is to be sure to EQ with the same microphone that the singer uses. This will help to identify the trouble frequencies that will confront you when you turn up the singer's mic. Embrace your identity by copying the singer.

"GRANDMA, WHAT BIG HIGHS YOU HAVE"

8/11/95 Van Halen

This topic has been touched on elsewhere but I would like to specifically focus on the importance of EQ'ing anything at the approximate level it will be during the show. Let's talk about general PA EQ'ing. If you EQ the PA at a quiet volume and then crank things up considerably during the show, you will most likely find that things will get pretty bright in some areas.

The same holds true when you EQ a vocal. If you try to keep things nice and peaceful during the day and EQ quietly, you will find that a smooth sounding vocal can get pretty biting when you turn it up. Instruments will also fool you if you EQ at the wrong level. Something that sounds big and fat can thin out when you turn it up, and conversely, a vocal that is EQ'd too loud will sound muddy when you turn it down. You must EQ things at the volume they will be at show time. When things are turned up they just naturally are accentuated in the high end. You would be surprised how many veteran sound engineers still get caught forgetting this. I constantly find myself trying to be considerate while I tune the PA and then getting caught with front fills or near fills being too loud when the show starts. You have to do your job, so try to pick a time when most of the people are having lunch or things are kind of slow in the activity department and let things rip.

If you are mixing a show where the volume level is quite low, you usually don't have to worry about annoying people. But don't get caught in the reverse trap and check your drums or other instruments at blazing levels that they won't ever get to during the show. Get a feeling for the level of your show from day to day and set up your channel and system EQ around this level. You will have to do so much less knob twisting come showtime and the start of your show will sound much better if you just remember this one rule. Also, speakers will be at safe levels and won't tear people's faces off with too much high end if you adhere to this. Don't let a gentle sounding soundcheck turn into a big bad wolf come show time.

"COME ON, WORK WITH ME HERE"

3/16/95 Van Halen

This is a little addendum to the previous note about working well together with your fellow sound guys. Here's a routine that I found to make the whole front-of-house EQ'ing of the vocal mic a more accurate representation of how it will be in the big picture.

It started every day by giving the monitor guy the time he needed to EQ the vocal mic on stage before ever turning it up in the main house speakers. Once he felt he had things pretty close, he would ask me if there were any frequencies coming off the stage by way of the wedges and sidefills that were causing a problem in the house. Now for all of you who are cracking up at all the love and concern for each other that is flowing here between this monitor guy and myself, let me just say that the results of working together in this manner were very successful.

If there were some low-end frequencies that were kind of sticking out in the house with only the monitor system on we would try notching out those frequencies on stage and then check if the feeling of fullness came back once the PA was turned on. If the monitors sounded thin after pulling out those frequencies even with the PA on, I would then suggest to the monitor guy that he put things back to where he needed them to be. By listening to what the other person was doing EQ-wise, we would know what cuts or boosts in different frequency areas were needed to make things work for both of us. If it helped him on stage to cut some things out in the house I would do that, with the agreement that if it hampered the outcome of what I was trying to do with the house EQ, we would find another compromise.

Another aspect of this is going up on stage and having someone at the house console turn the PA on and off while you talk into the vocal mic and listen to the monitors. You will get a better idea of what is happening on stage, and you may see that by cutting certain dominant frequencies you will make the singer, monitor guy, and probably yourself happier in the end. The out-front mix is a sum of all the parts and when you're EQ'ing anything you should listen at some point to those things with the monitors on. I like to listen to vocals and drums by themselves first but then I will always see what having the monitors turned on will do to the sound in the PA. Play together nicely and the sandbox will be a happier place for us all.

"BE A HIGH VOLUME DEALER"

8/18/97 Ted Nugent

When you are EQ'ing a PA, a monitor, or an instrument or voice through one of these speakers, be sure to pay attention to the volume at which you are listening as you tune. Be aware that things may sound drastically different at various volumes. You may be EQ'ing a vocal and find that as you begin at a low volume, things sound a bit muddy and lack crispness.

A lot of times the first instinct is to reach for the old graphic or channel EQ. Before you go there, ask yourself, "At what volume will this vocal potentially or nominally be throughout the show?" If the answer to that question is "a whole lot louder," then you will want to emulate that show volume as you tune. This isn't always the most pleasant thing for the people around you but hey, having a moving light focused in your eyes for 45 minutes isn't my idea of crew togetherness either. Anyway, the point is that to EQ at a much different level than show level can be a complete waste of time. If you want to know how it will sound for the show, you need to be in the ballpark of show level as you EQ.

There are a couple of reasons for this, and I'm not sure this book is the forum for getting to the technical reasons of why, but suffice it to say that our ears hear things differently at different levels, and PA speakers tend to change their tone in a non-linear way as the volume increases or decreases. (Whew!

That was very close to dancing on the edge of technical jargon). Conversely, if you are doing a show that tends to be quiet, you will shoot yourself in the foot if you are EQ'ing at warp drive levels. You can't always know in advance what the volume of the performance is going to be so sometimes you just have to guess and tune within your standard comfort zone for level. But whenever possible, estimate show level and go from there. You may find that once the PA is tuned at show level, turning up individual inputs in the mix will sound pretty darn good flat if you turn them up to the same show level. That's what to hope for, anyway.

CHAPTER 10

Delay Measurements

The notes in this book were collected over a span of seven or so years of touring. As I looked back over the notes for editing I discovered several ideas or theories that seemed rock solid several years ago didn't necessarily apply in the same way today. I updated those pages to reflect my new "modern" thinking.

Other notes were created on recent tours where my tuning processes didn't even resemble the way I did it just a few years ago. The bulk of these notes relate to delay measurements. Measuring components and zones of PA has been around far longer than the years this book has been in the creative stages, but touring audio companies and engineers have shied away from incorporating it into daily life until recently. With the increased use of computer measurement programs, separating your system into zones and time-aligning those zones has become much easier and accurate. The results have not been ignored by the knob-twisting masses. We all know the benefits of using delay to make the sections of our PA more coherent. Dive in and learn some of the techniques I have put to use to make the whole sound system sound more like one big happy stereo.

"IF YOU'VE GOT THE SPEAKERS, I'VE GOT THE TIME"

4/15/93 Van Halen

As you climb the audio ladder of success, you will often be called upon to perform tasks you never thought you would have to face. When you are a club mixer, you are seldom required to tie in to separate delay speakers for the purpose of sending sound reinforcement further than the main speakers will adequately cover. If you are not able to use a computer program for audio that calculates delay times for you, there is a formula that will quickly let you know the correct delay time for the second set of speakers. Our goal is to delay the sound from these speakers so that it lines up with the time it takes for the sound from the main speakers to arrive. Being that sound travels at 1100 feet per second in average environmental conditions (another long discussion), a set of delay speakers 200 feet from the main cluster must be delayed to keep everything time-aligned.

Many of the new delay devices around these days make this a very simple task, as all they ask you to do is insert the distance in feet (or yards or meters) and they do the calculation for you. This is fine until the time comes that you get a delay device that doesn't have this feature. The math that I do is a little bit of a rounding off process, but it serves the purpose of getting things fairly close time-wise. What you want to do is take the longest tape measure you can get your hands on and measure the distance between the main array of speakers and the next set of delay speakers.

Let's just say for example that the delay speakers are set up on a platform behind the mix riser at approximately 150 feet. What you want to do is take the distance between speakers and multiply that by .88 milliseconds (ms). In this example we have 150 x .88, which comes out to 132 ms. By setting the delay time of the second set of speakers at 132 ms, you can be assured that things will be pretty close. It's still a good idea after setting up delay times to check with a clicker, or make a "t" consonant sound with your voice, or even listen to the snare drum through the two sets of speakers. You should be able to hear an audible double attack effect if your delay time is not set correctly. If both sounds seem to occur at the same time, then you have things pretty much "ball-parked."

Remember that delaying speakers is a bit of an imperfect science, as only the seats that are located directly in line with the two sets of speakers hear the absolute correct delay time. Seats on either side will often hear a slight slap effect, as the delay will not quite line up for them. As always, use your best judgment. If the delay speakers are causing more harm than good, turn them way down, or off. If you desperately need top-end sound reinforcement to carry to the back of the room or outdoor area, then sacrifice a few weird out-of-time zones and go with the extra sound that will make the overall concert more appreciated.

"COMMON GROUND"

7/13/99 Luis Miguel

While we're on the subject of delayed rows of speakers, let's talk about delay times between zones of the PA. When you have two zones of PA (let's say for example the down fill of the main array and the front fill) overlapping in some seats, you will need to set the delay time of the one arriving first to coincide with the one arriving last. There are many methods to do this: a clicker or a measuring tape (by now a Stone Age technique) or a new-fangled analysis program like Smaart or IASYS.

Whatever your poison, you must decide which sections of seats you are choosing to align to. By this I mean there are always going to be some seats that are closer to one speaker zone than the other, and as you move out of that one speaker zone and into the next, the required time alignment would need to be different to completely be correct. Unfortunately, we live in a world of averages and not a world of perfection, and this definitely applies here. You want to find the common area where these zones overlap, and then pick a location for your mic or measuring tape that can identify the differential in time.

Common sense is really the only way to do this. In our example of the down fill and front fill—and for our example let's say you are using a measurement mic and Smaart to find delay times—you will want to place the mic in the center of the seats where these two zones overlap. One way to assist yourself in this endeavor is to run a little pink noise or music through each zone at an even level and then walk into the middle of the zones' overlapping area. You then want to have someone mute one zone for a second and then turn it back on for a second. Fading one zone in with volume while the other is already on is another good way to feel this out. You will get a feel for where the two zones overlap the most, and this is where you'll place the mic.

The methodology of time aligning the entire system is not the issue in this memo but only where to measure for the time differential. There will be another memo describing the entire time alignment process that works best later ("Draw it up align at a time," page 99). Find the common ground between your zones to avoid later problems that will require counseling and lawyers and litigation and ... Well, you know.

"DELAY YOUR ARRIVAL"

11/5/96 Julio Iglesias

It's true that we can't really have it all. Take for instance the first day a show goes on sale. Which tickets go first? The ones in the very front, of course.

Now here's the ironic part: The best seats from which to view a show are also the toughest seats to make sound good. It takes hard work and a flexible budget to make it great.

Having said all that, here is something to consider that raises the budget a little, but if you feel you need this little bit of extra polishing in your PA, it will make things sound much nicer for the highest paying folks right up front. When you put up front fill speakers, the ones that are intended to cover the seats right in front of the stage–the seats that never really hear the main focus of the house left and right PA speakers–it is important to remember that these speakers are going to be a lot closer to the audience members than the ones that are flown 20 feet in the air on each side of the stage.

The problem with this is that the sound from these front fills will arrive at these listener's ears quite a bit before the sound from the main speakers. This can be really confusing for the listener and it makes the show sound worse for these folks. To help combat this problem I suggest using a delay in line with the send to the front fill speaker amplifiers. By getting an average distance of discrepancy between the front fill speakers and the main speakers you can calculate an average delay time to apply to all your front fill speakers. It won't be perfect for all the seats up front because each seat in that area is a slightly different distance away from the mains, so an average is the best you can do. By applying the rule of delay time in relation to feet (approximately .88 ms per foot, see "Time is on your side" above) you can really fix up this section of the crowd. Getting the level to blend in with the main PA level and having the delay time right down there will give you this coherent feeling that you are really hearing the main PA speakers when you are actually hearing more of the front fills. By filling in just the missing upper frequencies in these front fills you will give great coverage up front without leaving the listeners with a feeling that they are swimming in slaps and reflections.

Some people prefer to fly a center cluster and point that down at the people up front and this sometimes works great, although it can cause feedback problems and confusion on stage for the artist, so I have found the front fill way works better for me. Whatever the method, I just want to clearly state that the toughest place to make sound good should get a little more attention than it does, seeing that those are the first tickets that sell. Even though the screaming is ten times louder than any speaker made, let's make our front fill speakers sing and reward our band's maniacal fans.

"DRAW IT UP ALIGN AT A TIME"

4/12/00 Luis Miguel

Okay, we've been dwelling on the subject of time alignment for the last couple of memos and it's now time to attack the whole process head on. As with everything in this book, this is the process that works best for me at the time of this writing. It may not be the best way for you, but in the most recent past, this has been the step-by-step method that has brought me the most success in relation to time aligning the whole PA.

Some things to get out of the way right away: If your PA system is not split up into zones (front fill, long throw, down fill) then you can't do much to get it all time aligned. If you don't have separate control (crossovers, EQ and delay) over each zone then the same applies. If you are lucky enough to own or rent a PA where you can have some control over the various zones, however, then here's the way I suggest you go about getting those zones time aligned.

A must-have device that will help you get everything in line is a computer-assisted "delay find" program like Smaart, SIM, or IASYS (and there are other great ones too). With these programs you are able to listen to one zone and let the computer store a distance between the source (the speaker) and the measurement mic. This makes things much easier than getting the old measuring tape out or "clicking" through two different zones and trying to match up the click in the time domain by ear.

Whatever method you can afford to own or the one that is available to you doesn't really matter, although realistically measuring the distance between the long throw speakers of your system and a mic at the back of the hall with a tape measure is not easy. The process to follow can be performed with any one of the above methods. I suggest and personally use the Smaart program and that is the way I will lay this out. The purpose of this is to get your entire PA time aligned to an average area so that there aren't two sources being heard in one area with different arrival times.

Here we go: Start by placing the measurement mic in a common area between the two zones that you are going to time align. (This is thoroughly discussed in "Common Ground.") Run some pink noise through the system with both the pink noise output and the microphone running into the computer to be analyzed. (The computer program's owner's manual should explain this method). Get a distance measurement (which you can convert to milliseconds if you prefer) of the one zone that is most likely a little further away in time than the other zone. Let's say you get a reading of 75 ms. Now you want to measure the distance (time) between the second zone and the mic. Follow the same method. Let's say you get a time of 70 ms because the speakers in this zone are slightly closer. Now you will want to add 5 ms of time to the zone that is closer so that the new reading on your computer will be 75 ms as well.

This method can be repeated for all the zones in your system. For example, put the mic down where the front fill and the main fill zones overlap. The front fill speaker should be closest so you will want to start by measuring the main zone. Then measure the front fill time and add enough to that to make it arrive at the same time as the main speakers. Get the picture?

It's not too tough a procedure. It's just having the tools that's the tough part. This works as well for delay systems. Put the mic out there where the delay speakers are aimed and then measure the distance from the main speakers and then the delay speaker and add time to the delay speakers. It works great and it's easy and your whole rig will sound so much better. Buy the program, any measurement program, and start getting proficient at this. For sub-bass delay, you can try all these methods but to date, I haven't found one that works with exact results.

The next memo, "sub-standards," explains a great procedure for finding the sub-bass delay time. As far as the rest of your PA, you can get things nicely aligned by following these methods. Remember to work in a pattern of setting times for the furthest speakers and then moving on to the next zone of speakers which are closer in distance. This way you are not changing a zone's delay time after it has been set. Time to align.

"SUB-STANDARDS"

3/18/00 Luis Miguel

Each and every section of the PA is important and necessary, but often the one that will make or break the overall sound is the sub-bass. It seems that all of us enjoy a good thumping sound and even in different lighter styles of music a solid foundation of low end smoothes out the overall sound. As audio manufacturers make their speakers better and better, it is easier to get a single box right off the shelf and plug it in and have it sound great. That is because within the cabinet itself the speakers are time aligned with each other (i.e. 15" lows are physically placed to be in time with the 12" mids and etc.). Also, the speaker system has a processor that comes as a part of the rig that has delay times for all the components, pre-determined to be most effective. This generally keeps the main PA time aligned unless the systems tech starts flying the individual cabinets incorrectly or stacking things without the front edges of the boxes lining up.

Keeping correct time alignment for an entire PA gets harder and harder as you multiply the amount of boxes and angles you are trying to cover, with more than one speaker pointing in one area. This is an area of discussion that requires a lot of time, has many possible angles, and demands many frosty malt beverages with your fellow debaters to resolve. Right now, the issue at hand is sub-bass time alignment. I have probably gained more practical knowledge in this area (to go along with the book learnin') in the past couple of years than in all my years of doing audio.

There are tools in almost any digital crossover now to do component time alignment and even if you don't have a new-fangled device like this in your system, you can use alternate, separate digital delays for reasonable amounts of money.

Now let's talk a little theory.

Hey! Where did you go? This is practical theory so you can come out now. Let's assume you have one of those new speaker boxes with the whiz-bang processor and you have your lows, mids and highs all time aligned within the box. If you do a ground stack and you place the high mid speakers on top of your subs you should be pretty close (in time) to correct. The problems start when you start flying the main speakers and ground stacking the subs. As you can guess, the physical location of the two sources of sound is different. In some sections of the house the distance between the subs and the main array may be exactly the same but usually the majority of the seats have a differential in arrival time of the two sources.

Here is where the delays come in handy. And here is where a little theory comes in. Some folks believe that the best way to align the two sources is to delay the subs until they couple up correctly with the rest of the PA. If you spin the delay time knob on your sub-bass digital delay you will find that you will eventually locate a time where the subs and 15's start to couple nicely. This may work but may not necessarily be the best method. The theory is that sub-bass frequencies take longer to develop and, therefore, delaying the subs makes the sound from the subs take even longer to get to the ear. A theory that was presented to me and only makes it into this book because it works more often than not is to delay the rest of the speakers to arrive at the same time as the subs. This has almost always worked to achieve a better kick drum sound and more coherent lows in the end.

If you are following my borrowed theory, what do you delay the main PA to? Over the years I've seen some sound companies and many individuals delay the PA speakers back to the guitar and bass speakers on stage or to the loudest low-end source on stage, which often times is the drum monitor. In most cases this can be up to 20 ms or more. If you don't go too much further than this you won't have a weird doubling effect between what the singer is singing and what he hears coming out of the speakers. Too much more than this can make it tough on him. Okay, so let's assume we move the 15's, 12's and 2's back digitally in time 20 ms. Now we want to time align the subs to the rest of the speakers. Like I mentioned earlier, it is never going to be the same everywhere in the house, so where is a good average location to time align to that is the center of most of the seats? The mix position often is just this. If you have a weird situation with a balcony in a theatre or a weird mix position you may want to choose a different location, but let's just say for grins that we will time align for front of house.

Assuming the other components are already time aligned we are trying to find the best time between the 15's and the sub-bass (let's assume they're 18's). You can make a logical guess at a starting point by visually estimating the difference in arrival time between the main array and the subs. Assuming we have the main array delayed at 20 ms, let's say that the subs are going to arrive five feet later than that or 5 ms roughly. Let's start then by delaying the subs 15 ms (so they arrive roughly five feet in time before the rest of the speakers, you still with me?) and go from there. If you want to start with pink noise, you will then open up the crossover on the subs and 15's; for starters only listen to one side of the PA. This method lets you listen to the two separate low-end components that will add or subtract frequencies based on your time aligning.

With the pink noise flowing through the 15's and subs, look on your Real Time Analyzer (if you have one) at the crossover frequency between the subs and 15's. Now mute the 15's. Does the crossover frequency increase or decrease in level when you do this? If it increases then you either want to start by flipping the subs 180 degrees in polarity, or your initial time alignment figure for the subs is way off. The goal is to have the subs and 15's add at the crossover frequency when they are both on. At this point you can just do some exploratory surgery. While listening to the pink noise, try moving the sub-bass delay time around between 0 and 20 ms. Start at 0 ms and then move up to 3 ms. Listen for a little bit. Did the level of coupling between the subs and 15's increase or decrease? Search around some more. Each time, give the pink noise a little time to settle in with the new delay setting and then listen.

You will find one or two spots that you really like and you will definitely find some that you know are wrong. When you find one you like, un-mute the other side of the PA and listen (again only to the subs and 15's). Do they continue to add? Great! Now, I suggest you use some other source to listen to. We use a thumper or popper that is used for checking phase on speakers. You may also want to try a DAT of your drummer's kick drum or the kick drum itself (but this takes a while and you need a patient drum tech). I like the thumper myself. Run this into a channel on your board a let it thump away. Again listen to the way the subs and 15's add. You will find at times that the subs take over and sound really big but the 15's sound wrong. Then you'll get a great chesty 15" sound but the subs will sound thin. The solution is somewhere in between, with the subs and 15's working together and coupling nicely with a good solid summing at the crossover point. I then like to walk around from center to the outer areas of the room, or into the seats and farther out, to see how it is everywhere in the room. It may add nicely at front of house with a certain delay time but not everywhere.

This is where you have to decide if the time that you used is best for the situation you are in. This procedure takes a little practice to get the hang of, but you will find that with some trial and error you will learn to easily discover the correct or best time for the day with little effort. Some days the rooms are easier than others, too. Some show the best time right away and some take a few tries. I know this has been a lot of information to grasp, but the results will be a great payoff. Of all the analysis programs out there for the average guy, most of them fail to provide enough solid information in the sub-bass region. I have had the pleasure of working with one of the best SIM engineers in the world and he has proven time and again that he can find the correct sub-bass delay times electronically, but this is the only person I have seen do this without necessarily relying on his ears. These methods may not be the best, or foolproof, but they have helped me immeasurably in the past year and I urge you to work at it. Again, you need the tools to do this but with those tools, I guarantee your results will improve.

"GET SMAART"

9/11/99 Luis Miguel

This book is not about theory, and it's not about particular product endorsements. There are, however, certain products that come along that make such a huge impact on the industry that they deserve mention. One such product is the JBL Smaart system. It's a newer, slimmer and much cheaper—but not necessarily better—version of the Meyer SIM system. These systems do a variety of functions, from frequency analysis using sources such as the output of the console (pre vs. post EQ) to curve display using a flat response microphone to look at what the EQ changes are doing in the real world.

Probably the best function of these systems is accurate time alignment of speakers without guesswork, tape measures, or clickers. As I have acquired more tenure in audio I have realized that time alignment of speakers is a very crucial element in providing unsmeared, coherent, in-phase sound to the venue. In the past we would use our ears and measuring devices like tape measures to ballpark in the delay settings and sometimes (probably five in ten) we would get pretty close, and not so often (maybe one in ten) we would nail it. Pretty close will help, yes, but dead on will make a world of difference. I have seen the SIM verification of this. By delaying the 15" speakers in a speaker cluster for example by only a fraction of a millisecond, the time smear effect (two similar sounds arriving at your ears at slightly different times) will vanish and the results will be amazing.

There are lots of different theories on this and I am sure my writing will take some criticism, but this book is about—and has always been about—what works for me. I have heard the proof and no one can convince me that getting delay times exactly right doesn't do amazing things to the overall sound.

In addition to delay times, SIM and Smaart will help you look at various zones in your speaker array and show you how frequencies are combining. Oftentimes, zones around the sides of the venue can stand to lose some of their low-end energy since there is so much coming off the main part of the PA; once combined with the main PA, these zones will sound perfectly full-range. By looking at the combination of the main PA zone and the side zone on the screen, you will be able to determine how much energy to lose from the side zone, and the result will still be a "flat" curve on your screen.

Now you say, "I've been EQ'ing all my life with just my ears and have done just fine, why do I need a computer to do my EQ'ing for me?" You don't need a piece of equipment to do anything in your place, but technology is now available to help us see potential problems that once made us say, "I know there is something weird going on, but pulling frequencies out just doesn't seem to be solving it." I say, use the technology to give you clues to trouble and then use your ears to verify the results. This is especially true as you are learning to use these systems. There will be quite a large learning curve so depend on your ears more in the beginning until you can be sure of the data and what it's telling you.

The world of audio is changing drastically. Digital consoles and speaker cabinets that produce amazing amounts of energy from tiny enclosures are appearing and blowing everyone away. I love a lot of the old-school methods and approaches, but I believe in using new advancements in technology to further my goal of providing the best sound possible to every seat in the house. Get Smaart (or SIM, or TEF, or any similar product) or get left behind. People are paying big money for ticket prices these days and most expect great sound. Isn't that we want to give them? I do.

PART FIVE: SOUNDCHECK

SOUNDCHECK

This is the real meat and potatoes part of your day. This is the time of day when the lighting guys are safely back in their bunks and the real audio can get done. The labor intensive part of the day is behind you now so it's time to wash up, dig in, and be the highly trained professional you are.

This chapter will cover a lot. There are notes on line checking in a safe and productive manner, lots of good stuff on EQ'ing instruments and vocals, and even more stuff relating to drums and the use of signal processing gear. "Soundcheck" encompasses everything from line checking the instruments with and without band techs, walking the room while the "roadie band" jams, and then checking the real guys when they arrive for the formal soundcheck. It's a large chunk of the afternoon and, in many cases, it's the first time you will be making most of the choices completely on your own.

On recent tours I have had a system engineer who works with me on many of the important decisions throughout the day. We often decide together where the PA will hang and how much we'll use, and in what configuration. Then we may tune the system together. In the cases where I have used a SIM engineer, he has used his measurement equipment to do much of the system level balancing and tuning on his own. But once the system is ready for some instruments and vocals to blast away, it's all about me.

This is when the instincts take over and you run on autopilot. All the shows you've done over the course of many years pile up in the form of experience and you just do what you do. I'll attempt to pass along many of those instincts here. This is where this book really began, in the day-to-day procedures that always took place while I soundchecked the instruments and the band. I hope you learn some stuff and find places to use these tips in your day.

CHAPTER 11

PFL (Pre-Fader Listen)

This chapter deals with the alternative ways to listen to instruments and vocals aside from letting them rock through the big speakers. Good old headphones or small monitor speakers can serve the great purpose of providing a more accurate way to listen to things, without outside noise and the reverberations in the room that may mask the true tonality of the instrument or vocal. They are often necessary to hear hums and buzzes and they can even be used as a safety measure to your ears and speakers to quietly listen to a problem that may scream through the PA if you turned it up.

I've included some of these safety tips as well as some good suggestions for using pre-fade listening to your advantage, and not your detriment. So, grab a set of cans, pull up an easy chair, and listen in.

"METERS FIRST, HEADPHONES SECOND"

9/14/95 Van Halen

One thing that can happen as we get into a daily routine on the road is that our safety awareness tends to diminish as each day passes without an injury. It's easy to blast our ears with too much level, either through the main speakers or our headphones, and we should always be aware that the potential is there to do damage. One way to give our ears a good thumping is during a line check when we have our headphones on. When we do a one-off we generally start off with a zeroed board and all gain settings must be set from scratch. This being the case, we are generally more careful of overcooked input levels coming to the board because we haven't heard the instrument through the rig in use before.

Whenever this is the situation, be sure to look at the input meter on your console, and set the input gain to a realistic setting before you reach for the headphones to listen to what's coming in. If you put your headphones on first, and then carelessly cue up the instrument without setting the gain first, you can give yourself a real blast. This danger does not surface as much when you are checking a band's inputs for the first time, because we are generally more aware that the potential problem exists. Where we get caught with this is during the day-to-day monotony of a touring show. We just assume that everything is the same as it was the show before and we go along cueing up channels in our headphones during the line check.

Now I will admit I've not been burned too many times with this, as things do tend to remain unchanged from show to show, but you never know when someone may have bumped a knob on your mixer when it was being set up, or a 20 dB pad may have been punched out by accident. This happened recently on an overhead cymbal channel. I cued it up with the pad out, and I think you can imagine how pleasant that was (ouch!). The good thing was I had it cued up in my console monitors only so I didn't get a direct shot to the eardrums. With these precautions in mind, be aware that things can change, and a good shot to your ears can cause permanent damage. Try to remember to look at the input meter or PFL first, and put your headphones on second. I also like to make a habit of turning the headphone/PFL level down to zero after listening in to protect myself next time around. Your ears are your gig, so protect them!

Tour: VAN HALEN 1998	Out Date 2/11/98

Ch.	DESCRIPTION	MIC	STAND	INSERT
1	O/H SR	AT4050		
2	O/H C	AT4050		
3	O/H SL	AT4050		
4	Ride	AT4041		
5	F2	ATM23		Gate
6	F1	ATM23		Gate
7	R2	ATM25		Gate
8	R1	ATM25		Gate
9	Hat	AT4041		
10	Snare 2	ATM23		Gate
11	Snare 1	ATM23		Gate
12	Kick SL 3	SM91	---	Gate
13	Kick SL 2	ATM25		Gate
14	Kick SL 1	AT4055		Gate
15	Kick SR 3	SM91	---	Gate
16	Kick SR 2	ATM25		Gate
17	Kick SR 1	AT4055		Gate
18	Bass DI 1	Countryman	---	Bass DI 1 Diredt Out: 120X-DS #2 Send
19	Bass DI 2	Countryman	---	
20	~~Bass FX L~~ 120x Bass	Countryman	---	
21	~~Bass FX R~~ 120x Drums	Counjtryman	---	
22	Gary Voc.	Radio		901-9098-TLA100
23	Gary Spare	Radio		901-9098-TLA100
24	JJ Voc.	AT4054		
25	Mike Voc.	AT4054		
26	EVH Voc.	AT4054		
27	EVH Piano Voc.	C535		
28	Guitar L Bright	SM57		
29	Guitar L Dark	Y from 28		
30	Guitar C Bright	SM57		
31	Guitar C Dark	Y from 28		
32	Guitar R Bright	SM57		
33	Guitar R Dark	Y from 28		
34	Guitar DI	Countryman	---	
35	Piano L	C414		
36	Piano R	C414		
37	Piano Pickup	BBE 4000XL	---	
38	Keys L	Countryman	---	
39	Keys R	Countryman	---	
40	Voc. Sample L	Countryman	---	
41	Voc. Sample R	Countryman	---	
42	TC 2290 L	---	---	
43	TC 2290 R	---	---	
44	H3000 L	---	---	
45	H3000 R	---	---	
46	M5000 A-L	---	---	
47	M5000 A-R	---	---	
48	M5000 B-L	---	---	
49	M5000 B-R	---	---	
50	224XL L	---	---	
51	224XL R	---	---	
52	Gary Wire	AT4054		
53	Acoustic Guitar	Countryman	---	
54		---	---	
55		---	---	
56	ProMix01 #1 Left	---	---	
57	ProMix01 #1 Right	---	---	
58	ProMix01 #2 Left	---	---	
59	ProMix01 #2 Right	---	---	

M.A. 3/24/98 10:01 AM

VCA	
1	Kicks & Snares
2	Toms
3	Cymbals
4	Bass
5	Guitar Dark
6	Guitar Bright
7	Keys
8	BGV
9	Gary Voc.

GROUP OUTPUT	
1	Drums L
2	Drums R
3	Bass L
4	Bass R
5	Keys L
6	Keys R
7	BGV L
8	BGV R
9	Gary Voc. L
10	Gary Voc. R

GROUP SUB-IN	
1	
2	
3	
4	
5	
6	
7	
8	
9	
10	

AUX OUTPUT	
1	224XL
2	SPX990 #1
3	SPX990 #2
4	SPX990 #3
5	SPX990 #4
6A	M5000 A
6B	M5000 B
7	H3000
8	TC2290
11	Dynacode
12	120X-DS #1

AUX SUB-IN	
1	
2	
3	
4	
5	
6A	
6B	
7	
8	
11	
12	

MATRIX OUTPUT	
1	Main System Left
2	Main System Right
3	Side Left / Front Fills
4	Side Right / Zone 8
5	Press Feed L
6	Press Feed R
7	Monitor L
8	Monitor R
9	Record L
10	Record R

MATRIX SUB IN	
1	
2	
3	
4	
5	
6	
7	
8	
9	
10	

GROUP INSERT	
1	
2	
3	Composer
4	Composer
5	Composer
6	Composer
7	Composer
8	Composer
9	
10	

AUX INSERT	
1	
2	
3	
4	
5	
6A	
6B	
7	
8	
11	
12	

This is a standard list on every tour. These come in all shapes and forms. Pertinent information includes snake line, front-of-house console channel, monitor console channel, and description of the input. Secondary information can include insert information like a gate or compressor, the type of mic used on that channel, and stage patch information such as the sub-box description.

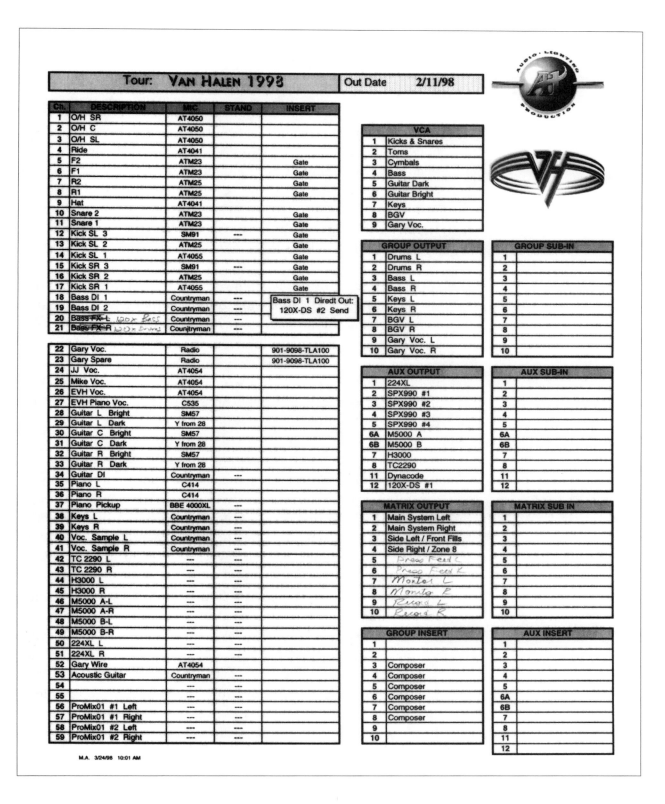

"I CAN ONLY LISTEN TO ONE OF YOU AT A TIME!"

6/8/94 Extreme

Whenever you cue something up in the headphones to give it a better listen, make sure you know what you're listening to. You need to listen to one thing at a time, so be certain that you only have the thing you are intending to listen to cued up by itself. This may seem a little elementary, but you would be surprised (and you could probably tell a horror story or two yourself) by the confusing problems that can arise from not being careful.

A good example of this is when you are doing a line check and you cue up the bass guitar only to find there is a buzz on that channel. Some sound guys like to move on and come back to buzz problems later, after you have finished the general task of making sure you have all your lines. If you forget to un-solo the bass guitar channel and then cue up a keyboard channel, followed by the vocal channel, you may fully believe that every channel you're listening to is buzzing.

Now, this may seem like something so stupid that you would never do it. I would, however, have to raise my hand as guilty several times in my career for doing this exact thing. A more common mistake that occurs (and much less easy to catch) is cueing up a tom mic or an overhead cymbal mic and forgetting to un-cue it. You then listen to a vocal or kick drum mic and hear a lot of ambience or ringing (in the case of a tom mic that's left cued up), and you think that the vocal or kick drum is the thing that sounds strange. A lot of consoles have addressed this problem by having a light that indicates when you have a PFL or AFL engaged, which lets you know you have left something cued up. This usually happens when you are moving quickly in the heat of battle and you forget to un-solo something. Then, if you don't cue up the next thing in the headphones for a long while, you forget to disengage the last thing you had cued up.

This may seem like a fairly unimportant little bit of information, but if you develop a bad habit of doing this, I can guarantee it will jump up and grab you somewhere down the road.

6/22/93 Van Halen

Sometimes when you do a string of one-off shows, the quality control is much better than when you are on a tour and well into the sixth or seventh month. There is much to be said for getting in a groove and finding a routine that works well for the whole crew, but the problems will start when you've been clipping along for weeks without a major problem and everyone starts to feel invincible.

It's about this time that line checks start to become a little too relaxed and things get overlooked. I find myself looking at the meter bridge waiting for the keyboard player/tech to start playing. When I see level coming at me that looks correct, I'll turn up the keys and have a listen in the PA, shut them off and tell the keyboard player that all is well. The thing being missed here is not checking the line in your headphones or console monitors before turning it up in the PA. The reason for this is that some rooms mask the source sound by means of long reverb times or strange reflections and characteristics. There might be a slight distortion on one of the lines or some other type of abnormality that might get missed by just listening through the PA. Check out the sound in your headphones before you turn the PA on to reference things to the way they've always sounded.

At this point it's good to have the player stop (or even before they start playing), and have a good listen down the lines in your headphones for any buzzes or hums that may be present on the line. It's also a good idea to listen to the channel through the PA with nothing coming through it to check for buzzes. There's nothing worse than doing a line check and thinking everything is fine, only to find that when the band shows up, and you turn all the channels on, things are buzzing wildly. Use your head and your headphones to ensure good clean, buzz free inputs that sound like they did yesterday. Things will sound different from day to day in the room you are mixing, but they should sound almost identical in your headphones each day.

CHAPTER 12

Equalizing Instruments and Vocals

If you tuned your PA effectively, this can sometimes be the easiest part of your day. In a good sounding room with a nice "flat" sound system, you will often find you turn instruments up and they sound good from the get-go. The right mic plays a great part in this as well.

The reality of most days is that you'll have to grab the knobs and sort out some problem frequency areas with some of your instruments and vocals. No biggie! Here are some pointers to help you swim to the deep end without your "floaties." You'll thrill and amaze your friends and cohorts as you skillfully twist knobs and make nasty frequencies disappear like magic. There really are some tricks to this, so stay tuned.

Hey, no peeking behind the curtain.

"GET YOUR SELECTIONS IN EARLY"

5/13/93 Van Halen

A trick I like to use in regards to parametric EQ has to do with being prepared. When you do your soundcheck be aware of the dominant frequencies in the various instruments and vocals you are listening to. In kick drums, you will want to find the frequency that gives you the best attack or snap at the top end; then, locate the midrange frequency that makes the drum sound boxy. After that you will want to locate the low-end frequency that gives it the best thump, as well as the width of "Q" to use. Then, simply listen to the drum through the PA with flat EQ. You may decide that none of the above frequencies that you located need to be boosted or cut at all because the drum sounds good perfectly flat. If that is true, you've obviously had the drum tuned well and chosen good microphones for your purposes. But if you have the time, sweep through each band of frequencies (low, low-mid, high...etc) and locate some key frequencies to either cut or boost.

The point here is that when you are in the heat of battle during the show and that drum starts to sound boxy, you've already got that frequency selected, just waiting to boost or cut. This routine holds true for everything. Find the hot spots in the keyboard channels. Find out what frequency to boost at the top to give it a nice sizzle if you need that. You get the picture. If you are on a mixing console for the first time (possibly in a one-off festival situation), you are not always going to have the time to do this. What you can do is prepare for the anticipated cuts and boosts by going with your experience and setting the EQ knobs to the frequencies you assume will be troublesome or helpful. Any time you can, your channels should be set up so that each band of EQ for each instrument or vocal represents a frequency that you might have to boost or cut during the show.

Instrument Pre-selected EQ Examples:

Instrument	Lo Freq Boost/Cut	Lo-Mid Freq Boost/Cut	Hi-Mid Freq Boost/Cut	High Freq Boost/Cut	General notes
Vocal	80 Hz/Cut	200-400Hz/Cut	2.5kHz/Cut	14kHz/Boost	Different voices require vastly different EQs but these settings give a good start
Guitar	60 Hz/Cut	400-700Hz/Boost	2.5kHz/Cut	6kHz/Cut	Clean and dirty sounds will change these These are set for grunge sound
Bass Guitar	100Hz/Cut	160-320Hz/Cut	1.6kHz/Boost	6KHz/Cut	Lower frequencies will shift a lot depending on the room, PA, and instrument's sound
Kick Drum	40Hz/Boost	200Hz/Cut	1kHz/Cut	6kHz/Boost	A well tuned PA will not require much unless the drum is not well tuned
Snare Drum	80Hz/Cut	400-630Hz/Boost	1.6-3.15kHz/Boost	8kHz/Boost	This all depends on how you like a snare to sound

This is not the ultimate instrument frequencies charts, but a rough idea of where you might want to pre-set your instrument's EQ knobs for possible adjustment during the show. With knobs pre-selected, you can simply reach for the cut/boost knob and spin away without having to spend too much time searching.

4/23/93 Van Halen

Here's a simple little procedure that will help you accurately locate troublesome frequencies to be removed or the best tonal characteristics to be boosted. This is one of those things I had people suggest I try for quite some time. When I did, I wondered how I'd ever EQ'd before. This method will only work if your mixing console's channel EQ is parametric (meaning you can select the frequency you wish to alter as well as the width of cut or boost you want to apply).

In this day and age, if you are using a mixer without at least a couple of frequency sections equipped with parametric EQ, you are indeed unfortunate, and braver than most of us who call ourselves pros. Let's say you are annoyed by a high-endy frequency in the guitar channel. You know that the frequency is around 2 kHz but you want to be a little more accurate. What you would do is this: Begin by going for the high-mid portion of your channel EQ (I'm assuming you have four-band parametric. If you only have three-band, then go for the mid band). What you want to do first is grab the bandwidth control knob, also known as the "Q" knob on some boards, and rotate it to the narrowest bandwidth that you can. Next you want to boost about 6 dB of gain in the area in which you are trying to locate the frequency (in our case we are looking to get rid of something around 2 kHz). Be sure to bring the fader level down a little bit before starting this last procedure if you want to have any dinner partners for the rest of the tour.

From here, you want to grab the frequency select knob, and with that 6 dB of boost in this general area, you want to begin sweeping through the frequencies in the 2 kHz area. You will usually discover very quickly which frequency is the one causing the trouble. Your next move is to decide if you only want to take out that particular narrow band of frequencies or a wider chunk. This is where you use the parametric EQ to shape your sound. Sometimes a little cut with a wider bandwidth of frequencies is the ticket and other times you just need to lose one particular frequency. In this instance, keep the bandwidth tight and cut a little more of just this one frequency. Use this method whenever you need to locate a frequency. Don't just guess. Accuracy in your frequency selections will pay off.

"GET YOUR HANDS OFF MY EQ"

4/29/93 Van Halen

One of the best tricks I have discovered has to do with guitar miking, and I don't mix a show without using this almost every second along the way. I'll first explain the procedure and then elaborate with some applications.

Depending on the setup of the guitar rig, there are several options for mic placement and actual numbers of mics, but that will be discussed later in the applications part. Here's one method: Let's say the guitar rig is set up with a three-cabinet system: left and right wet (effects) cabinets and a center dry cabinet (no effects). I like to EQ the center cabinet mic a little bright by taking out some of the low end; then, I EQ the left and right cabinet mics a little dull with some of the high end rolled off. After that I pan the left and right dull mics hard left and right and leave the bright center mic panned straight up. What this allows me to do is to simply move faders up and down to achieve the correct levels of cut or chunk as is needed within the context of the song. During the rhythm sections of the song, when the general guitar tone is chunky and sometimes a little bit dull and muddy, I will bring down the left and right faders a little and bring up the center mic (which is EQ'd bright) to allow the guitar part to cut through better.

Alternately, when the guitar player goes into a solo and starts playing up high on the neck, the tone of the guitar sometimes gets scratchy and bitey. When this happens I bring down the center mic and push the left and right faders to make the single string being played sound thicker and smoother. The old-fashioned way to do this would be to simply have a left and right pair of mics and re-EQ as the tone of the guitar changes, but the amount of EQ adjusting required during various parts of the song is overwhelming. My method seems to be much easier.

Another asset to this system is that when the guitar player goes into a solo and his sound thins out, boosting the left and right effects mics helps the solo seem thicker and wider. This is because the dull mics are panned hard left and right and the solo will get much larger in the stereo image. This method also helps out with tone changes by the guitar player as he switches from clean to dirty sounds on his pedalboard. Some clean sounds have a glassy top end that can get very bright in a reverberant room, and instead of reaching for the EQ you simply have to move the dull mics up and the bright one down.

Another more recent method involves "Y-ing" each of the three mics into two channels, which gives you six inputs: two wet-Left, two dry-Center, and two wet-Right. If you EQ one bright and the other dark for each of the three mics, and assign all the bright mics to one VCA and all the dark mics to another VCA, you can keep two fingers on two VCA's throughout the show and control the guitar tone. Try it and you will see that the ease of this system will be astonishing. Listening to any one of the mics by itself will probably sound quite strange, either too dull or too bright. But the combination of all of them should be an accurate representation of the real sound. By finding the balance of bright mics to dark mics you will find the starting point from which you can make your fader adjustments during the show.

Now, let's discuss other options that come from different guitar and PA setups. The above-mentioned setup is a three-cabinet stereo guitar setup run through a stereo PA system. This is not always the situation. If the guitar player is only playing through two cabinets—one dry and one wet—the best way to approach this is to use your left and right effects mics on the one effects cabinet and your center mic on the dry cabinet. The same panning of the left-right dull mics and the center bright mic still apply. If the PA you're mixing on is set up in mono, you will only need two mics with the above guitar rig: one EQ'd dull for the effects and one EQ'd bright for the dry cabinet, and there will be no left-right panning necessary.

If the guitar player has a setup with two cabinets, one effects left and one effects right, then you have a decision to make. The mics with dull EQ for the left and right effects will be as before, but the center bright mic must come from either the left or right effects cabinet. This will undoubtedly make your stereo imaging a little lopsided. What I have done in this situation is actually use four mics: left and right dull, and left and right bright, or use the dual VCA and "Y" method. The four-mic method is bordering on overkill and it's tough to keep four fingers on guitar channel faders at one time, so the dual VCA method seems best. If the guitar rig is a very simple one-cabinet setup where the effects are just layered over the dry sounds and everything comes through the one cabinet, I still suggest using three mics as described in the first situation; left-right dull and center bright. This will allow you to pan the left and right dull for a wider stereo image and have the center mic for your cut.

There will always be other guitar rig setups, but I've covered some of the possibilities, and the main point is to have tonal flexibility through different EQ settings. Another option is to choose different sounding mics for your bright and dull sounds. In a rock band situation I find myself mixing with my right index finger on the lead vocal fader and three fingers of my left hand on the three guitar channels or two VCA's. I rarely have to reach for EQ on those guitar channels and that frees me up for other things.

"WOULD THE REAL MUSICIAN PLEASE SPEAK UP"

6/14/94 Extreme

We all have specific characteristics in our voices, and if that is the tool you use to tune the PA, keep in mind that the predominant frequencies in your voice may be quite different from that of the vocalist in the band you are mixing. I'm not saying you shouldn't use this method to tune a sound system, as it is a very good way to get the overall EQ balance and feel out the reverb time and characteristics of the room.

Keep in the back of your mind though that the loudest thing in the PA is usually the singer's voice, so the tonal shaping of the EQ should fit the singer's tone and not necessarily yours (or the monitor guy's) when you ring things out. The trick is to recognize and try to put to memory the subtle differences between your voice and the singer's, and let this be a factor as you go along. This also holds true for getting drum sounds in the PA and monitors. Learn the difference between the hitting strength and style of the drummer and the drum tech. Sometimes you will add a lot of top end to the kick drum because the drum tech has a weak foot, and then the drummer comes in for soundcheck and sends pieces of titanium flying out of your high-end speakers when he thunder-foots the kick drum. The best thing to do in the case of instruments is to try to get the band techs to play as accurately as possible like the artist they are working for, so you can develop a correct soundchecking reference. This is not always possible, but in a perfect world the backline guys will give it their best shot.

In the case of singers, this is nearly impossible, so just attempt to develop a sense for what is needed EQ-wise in your own voice to make it sound like the singer's voice. I can personally attest to being unable to sing, so my tonal copycatting is limited to emulating frequency response in the singer's mic only. If this is the best you can do, then forge ahead. It's a far sight better than just yelling "one, two" into the mic and calling it a day.

"IF YOU MOVE IT AN INCH, IT CAN SOUND LIKE A MILE"

7/15/93 Van Halen

Miking is a very important element in what we do as sound engineers. It is the first link between the artist's instrument and the processes we apply to amplify that instrument. The right choice of mic for each of the different instruments and knowledge of how to best place that mic will get the best result. Some engineers like to use the same mics on certain instruments no matter who the artist is or what the style of music might be. This is usually done because they are so used to the way that specific mic sounds that they can do their best work with a familiar tool.

One facet of miking that is so very important is mic placement. We don't always have the time on a live show to move mics around to find the sweet spot of a drum or guitar amp like they do in the studio, but experience will teach you the best starting points for various instruments. With guitar amps, moving the mic around to different areas of the speaker cone will give you amazing variation in tone. Decide what works best for your application, and then lock that mic stand down so it doesn't get moved. I am amazed at how many times I see a show, especially in one-off situations where the sound engineer is unfamiliar with the band, and the sound man never gets near the stage to check the way the mics are placed before soundcheck.

I must say that during a rushed day at a music festival (or similar chaotic surrounding) I have been just as guilty as the next guy has. But it is really vital to check where the mics are pointed before you start listening, and then give the mic stands a good tightening so things won't be swinging around. After soundcheck, before the show, and immediately following the final opening act, you should make one more trip around the stage to make sure things haven't moved around. Making sure the mics stay pointed where you intended is a crucial step in keeping the sound you've EQ'd consistent. Don't settle for loose mic stands and be personally accountable for each mic's position by double-checking.

"I'VE DUG A HOLE AND I CAN'T GET OUT"

6/12/93 Van Halen

EQ: Friend or foe?

This has been pondered many times as we've reached for that knob or slider. If you've worked for the same act or show for a long time, you will find a certain EQ that sounded good at one time just isn't cutting it anymore. You add a little more of this, and cut a little more of that, and then everything theoretically sounds a little better.

I've seen channel EQ where all four bands are boosted or cut more than 6 or 9 dB. What are you really saying about the sound of that instrument or vocal? What works well in this situation is getting back to ground zero (0 dB of boost or cut that is). If you find that you've boosted all four bands of a channel quite a lot, try flattening all four boost knobs and then turn up the gain. From this new starting point you might need to add just a touch of one or two of the four bands and maybe cut a little of another. The old EQ might have been what you'd been looking for, but you've found yourself in an EQ war you can't escape from.

The same is true for system EQ. You may find that your system's main EQ looks more like a photo of the Rocky Mountains than the way it did when you pulled it out of the box. Flat EQ is not necessarily the answer, but a start to getting back on track. Start by flattening your graphic or parametric EQ, but be careful, as if your EQ was pretty cut up you'll now have a considerable gain increase. Then, use whatever method you use to retune the PA. You may have to adjust crossover levels with this new flat graph, but that's Ok. Get the system sounding as good as you can with a completely flat graph and then notch out a few hot spots here and there. This is something that needs to be done periodically. It will help with your gain structure and keep things running smoother.

Before you reach for the EQ, remember to ponder some other options. You may not have the best mic for the job on certain instruments, or your crossover settings may be unbalanced. One common mistake is to have certain zones of the PA louder than they should be, or certain components, such as the low mids, turned up too loud in the offstage zone of the PA. EQ is a very handy tool and very few PAs will sound exactly right from day to day without a touch up. But use it wisely, and it can be your friend instead of your foe.

"DRUMMERS AND GUITAR PLAYERS, LEND ME YOUR EAR"

4/16/95 Van Halen

It's easy to fall into the trap of thinking that the sound coming out of a guitar player's speakers at the microphone is exactly the tone he is trying to achieve. It may be closer to the truth to say that most of us don't know what the guitar sound is like right at the point where the speaker meets the microphone because we usually don't stick our heads that close to a screaming speaker. All we have as a reference is the sound that reaches our console through the mic.

What the guitar player usually perceives as his sound is the tone that meets his ears at the place where he stands, or the pocket he moves around in for most of the show. He generally will make tonal changes and level adjustments to the amp controls to please his ears, which are at a much greater distance from the speakers than where the mics are placed. For this reason it is not enough to simply turn up the guitar mics in the PA, and upon discovering the sound is not quite right say, "this is how he wants his rig to sound or he wouldn't have EQ'd his guitar speakers this way."

What you should do, especially the first few times you are soundchecking a new band, is walk up on stage and have a listen to how the rig sounds from where he is hearing it. It is usually considerably darker and warmer than what is going into those guitar mics. If you only have to move the position of the guitar mics in relation to the speakers, then your life is easy and you're done. More likely you will have to also go back to the mixing board and EQ a little bit until things sound more like they did on stage. The point is that the guitar player has spent countless hours getting the sounds he wants from his guitar rig, and if you were to ask him how he wants his guitar to sound, he would most likely ask you to come on up and have a listen. So it's a good idea to beat him to the punch and get an earful of what he is hearing, so you have the reference to make his guitar sound the same through the PA as it does on stage.

The same holds true for drums. Many times engineers will EQ drum channels before they ever hear the drum through the PA, because certain boosts and cuts of EQ on drums generally get things sounding about right. This is OK if you don't have the time to catch all the subtle nuances of the drum's tones, but like the guitar rig, drums have certain characteristics that might not be heard through each mic. Walk up behind the drum kit when someone is playing it and see how it sounds as a kit. Then, when you go back to the board you may decide to try some different mics, or looser gates, or some other options to make that drum kit sound a little closer to the way it does on stage.

We don't all get the luxury of spending time on this, and you are right in thinking that we often have to simply spin up some kind of sound from horrible sounding guitar rigs and drum kits just to get through the gig. This all may be true, but giving the players the benefit of the doubt that they know how their instruments should sound will help you to understand what they may be looking for. Then, when they say something is just not quite right, you may agree.

CHAPTER 13

Thinking It Through

Okay, you didn't get this job without showing some level of cranial prowess. If you don't know what I'm talking about maybe you didn't get the job. Anyway, when all the teaching is done and all the gear is up and working, there comes a time when you're going to have to rely on good old common sense and experience to turn it all into something great.

There's a good reason most students don't come right out of the classroom and mix up a storm their first time out. It's all about the hours logged in the saddle and piles of intellectual data to draw from, the old "been here, heard that" philosophy. After a while you'll recognize that you've walked down this road before and there's a big hole over there you shouldn't step into.

Read on to learn about some of the detours I've taken to avoid the potholes and make the big day a sweet drive on a freshly paved freeway.

"DO IT LIKE YOU DID IT LAST NIGHT"

8/18/95 Van Halen

A lot of times in this business, we will do more than one show in the same venue on consecutive nights. You may have discovered that during the soundcheck on the afternoon of the first show things sounded one way, and then as the show started and the place was full of sweaty bodies and smoke and noise, everything sounded considerably different. This is no great revelation. Venues very seldom sound the same at show time as they did in soundcheck.

It's hard to guess what acoustic changes are going to occur, so I've spent my career just going with the flow. By that I mean that at soundcheck I do the necessary things to make it sound right at that time, and then if I need to change things once the show has started, I make those necessary changes. I don't try to guess too much because I've guessed wrong enough times and have learned from my mistakes. I don't second-guess the surrounding situations. I just mix.

Having said all that, let me totally contradict myself in the instance of a second day in the same venue soundcheck. Some bands will have a great show the first night and still want to come in for a soundcheck the second day. I say if that makes you happy, go for it. If I was a musician in similar situations I'd rather play golf, but I'm a soundman and so I'll just stay out of that one. If the band does decide to come in, or if you are just line checking the instruments and vocals for a second time, be wary of making changes to compensate for the changed environment of the empty hall that second day.

Remind yourself that by the end of that first performance you probably had things sounding the best you could for that room with the crowd in it. Things might sound very different that second day with an empty room. By all means work on sounds if you weren't happy with them the night before, but if you were fairly happy with your mix last night, and the room sounds weird to you today now that it's empty, have no fear. Things will most likely be back to the way they were last night once everyone is in again. Just ride out the soundcheck even if things sound a little odd. They'll probably sound just right when the show begins. And be sure to explain this to the band so you can get your game of golf in.

"TO SOUNDCHECK OR NOT TO SOUNDCHECK"

12/30/93 Ted Nugent

The style of venue, the temperature of the venue, and how many tickets are sold can make the sound during soundcheck feel vastly different from the sound at show time. So then, how seriously do I value the levels and tones that I hear at sound-check and how much should I change the PA's EQ based on what I hear in the afternoon?

I must cheat on this question a bit and say that only experience will let you know how much to base system EQ on the soundcheck. I have personally found that if you are doing the same types of venue day in and day out you are probably better off leaving the system's EQ mostly untouched when you get into a new venue. This may sound rather radical at first, but you should only leave your settings if you are playing the same types of venue. I believe the greater difference in perceived sound is often an empty venue at soundcheck compared to the same venue after it is full, not necessarily a full venue from one night versus a completely different full venue the next night.

Again, I base this on experience and you may find that you perceive something to be completely different. What I have found is that I sometimes chase my tail in soundcheck trying to EQ the PA for a particular empty venue. I then observe midway through the show that my system EQ curve is closer to the way it was last night than the way it was at soundcheck.

So then, based on this information, do you soundcheck? Well, most of the time it isn't your choice anyway. Even bands that are just for hire, like a band backing a main vocalist of importance, may want to soundcheck every day even if the star doesn't come in. And I would recommend this for making the band feel comfortable with their monitors and surroundings. I like to use this time to walk around the venue with the instrumentation (or the whole band, vocals included) cranking away at near show level. This helps me get a last minute check of general level of my various zones of PA and a rough EQ estimate. So, based on this I say let the soundcheck happen even if that choice is in your hands.

When don't I like to do a soundcheck? When I'm playing multiple dates in the same venue and the band had a slamming night on night one. They almost certainly will feel like things are all wrong if they come in on day two when the venue is empty and the vibe is completely different. If you have a choice on day two, say no. I would line check and run a song through the PA to walk the room and make sure all speakers are working, and then check tuning on the drums, but don't start fiddling with the EQ if things were great the night before. If the band does insist on coming in and they give you the "it doesn't sound like last night" thing, gently point out that the conditions currently are nothing like last night and if they will just have some faith, things will feel much better when the place fills up.

I try very hard not to get the band to change everything from day to day. If you get on a routine with your band of not soundchecking, I have found that the number of changes they want in their monitors drops drastically. This is because they are always basing things on a full house and showtime temperature. If they routinely come in for soundcheck they may always be looking for changes in the day and then going back for something else at showtime. If they figure this out on their own they may stop the vicious cycle themselves.

"SET IT UP BUT LEAVE IT OUT"

5/14/94 Extreme

When you're doing a one-off or setting up your console and mix with a new system, be sure to keep it simple at first. Take advantage of time after your quick line check to get a few compressors and gate settings dialed in while the monitor guy is getting levels on stage. (See "Time is on your side," page 72.") Even if you feel like you've dialed in your compressor and gate settings in the headphones while line checking or during the monitor guy's EQ time on stage, leave the compressors and gates in the bypass position until you have had a chance to listen to the input in question.

If it is a vocal you're getting a level for or EQ'ing, be sure to listen with the compressor in the bypass mode before you start twisting knobs. The reason for this is that in a perfect world compressors would just control level and leave the pure tone of what you put in untouched, but this is not always the case. You may experience a noticeable difference in top end and overall tone once you insert the compressor, so begin with the bypass switch in and set your EQ and gain level accordingly.

The same goes for getting drum gates set up. Have a listen to the drum with the gate out, and then use the gate efficiently as a control device to tailor your sound, but get the sound and level set first. As for vocals and instruments that use compression, I would go so far as to say that when you're doing a one-off with a system you're not familiar with or that you haven't had lots of time to soundcheck and listen to, it is wise to start the show with the compressors on the instruments and vocals in the bypass position. The only exception may be a very erratic lead vocal. Get your mix happening and some EQ set on your main instruments and vocals and then bring in some compression to help with level control.

If you insist on using compression, then be sure that you are not slamming the threshold as the show starts and compressing things 10 or 12 dB, as this will back you into a corner. If you must leave the compressors in, be sure immediately that you are only compressing a little bit and then go to the EQ and find what you like. As far as gates go, I would always suggest starting with the gates in if you have set them well during line check or soundcheck. The last thing you want is a drum kit that is ringing all over itself. Keep it simple to start off.

CHAPTER 14

Working with Drums

Some may wonder why an entire chapter would deal strictly with drums. The answer is best described with one word: foundation. In order for a musical mix to have impact of any kind, there needs to be an underlying foundation that holds it all together. In pop and rock and roll music, the drums are often that foundation.

We spend a lot of time selecting mics, playing with gates and compressors, fiddling with mic positions, and finally pulling our hair out looking for the elusive "magical" drum sound. There have been days when we've approached it, and maybe a moment or two when the clouds have parted, the heavenly choir took to singing, and the goal was achieved. (At least until the snare went out of tune again.) But it can happen. We hear it often on the radio and on CDs. But live, it's another story. There are more tricks to getting a kickin' drum sound than can ever be taught in school, so here are a few of the things I've found to work over the years. I hope you gain some insights to achieve your drum nirvana.

"OPEN-MINDED"

6/23/93 Van Halen

I discussed before the effects of combined mics on a single instrument. In that example we talked about the snare drum. With the rack tom mics pointing down at the snare, I shed some light on how these tom mics also pick up the snare and can change its sound when they are turned on. This brings up the question of gating tom mics. If you can manage to get your tom gates to stay closed on every snare shot and still open up on cue with a light tap on the tom-tom, then you have done well. If this is the case, you can feel free to EQ the snare by itself and not have to worry about the tom mics altering the sound. If you can't seem to keep the tom gates closed consistently on the loud snare hits (join the club) I would suggest you loosen them up enough so that they will not partially open and close on snare hits as this gives a very strange attack EQ on the snare.

It is better to have smooth openings and closings of tom gates and allow for the EQ of the toms to combine with the EQ of the snare. This gives you a package EQ rather than having a changing situation moment to moment. Loud tom mics can greatly affect the EQ properties of the snare. Remember to incorporate the EQ of the tom mics into your snare EQ and then live with a slight opening and closing of gates. Your main consideration should be deciding if you're going to be able to keep those gates closed or not and then adjust EQ accordingly.

"BE CAREFUL, EVERYONE IS LISTENING"

6/28/93 Van Halen

Most instrument or vocal mics that are on a rock/pop music stage are generally pointing at the single source sound it is designated to amplify. In other words, a lead singer's microphone is used only to amplify that vocal through the PA system. It may pick up stage sounds such as guitar and cymbals, but its primary responsibility and input is the vocal. This holds true for guitar mics as well. The level into the mic is usually loud enough so that leakage from other instruments and unwanted sounds are not a problem.

This is generally not the case with drums. As soon as you start putting up tom mics, and overheads to pick up the cymbals, you create a situation where many microphones are pointing at the same drums. Although some of these mics are further away than the primary mic intended for each drum, and some of these mics are EQ'd so that the low end is rolled off, you still must consider the effect they will have when all mics are on at the same time. Just as two drums resonating simultaneously will affect the sound of a single drum, a similar situation occurs with microphone position. As mentioned in another memo, listening to a snare drum by itself may sound quite different from listening to the snare with the tom mics turned on, because the snare pitch may set off a ring in the tom.

The situation I'm describing here is similar, but involves multiple mics pointing at a single instrument. Let's look at a snare drum again. When you listen to the snare drum by itself you will adjust your EQ to get the desired sound you are looking for. If you then mute the snare channel(s) and go on to the toms, doing each one separately, you will arrive at a point where each drum sound by itself is what you're after. Now look at the position of the mics that you have for the rack toms. In most situations they are over the drum itself pointing down at the tom. If you will notice, it is most likely pointing at the snare also, but further away than the top snare mic. Now, while listening to the snare by itself, turn on one or two of the rack tom mics and see if any change in the sound of the snare occurs. It often will, especially if you like to have your toms quite loud in the mix. The reason is clearly that you have two mics pointing in the same general direction and the EQ and pickup patterns of the two mics will combine to give you the sound of your snare. Also playing a role is the discrepancy in arrival times the acoustic snare sound has into the two mics.

The same thing may occur when you turn on the overhead mics that are set up for your cymbal sound. The snare may have a little more top end when the overheads are on, rather than when they are muted. Now, this is not a cause for concern and it may even help you out. In the studio, combined microphones often make the overall drum sound bigger. In live sound, we tend to want to exclude everything except closely miked source sound, but sometimes the combined sound is better than the original. The main point here is to simply be aware of the combined effect. Depending on the location of snare and rack tom mics, you may find you get a better combined sound if one or more of the tom mics are out of phase with the snare mic. Remember after your individual drum channel EQ'ing is done to add the other drum channels and listen to the combined sounds. You may have to make slight EQ changes to some of the drums to make everything work together. Is everybody listening?

7/17/93 Van Halen

Drum tuning is an integral part of having a clean, tight mix. If you have a cool drum tech and/or a co-operative drummer, then you can implore them to be a part of the "tuning for the PA" process, a win-win situation for everyone in the end. The goal is to be sure that the pitches of the various drums are independent of each other. Often, the pitch that the snare is tuned to will set a tom ringing, or a similar situation will happen between the kick drum and floor toms.

A good way to check this is during your soundcheck, before the whole band is on stage. After getting the various levels and sounds on the drums, have the drummer/tech hit the snare and turn the toms up one at a time 5 or 10 dB louder than you will be running them at show time. If the snare causes a ring in one of the rack toms, a slight retuning of that tom (or snare) should clear things up. The same procedure should be used to check the floor toms. Hitting the bass drum and turning up the floor toms one at a time should determine whether a tuning change is necessary for one or both of the floor toms. It's not always the easiest thing to convince some drummers to retune their toms, but if you assure them (or let them hear for themselves) that it only takes a slight alteration to the pitch of the drum to clear up the problem they will very often oblige, especially if the separation of the drums cleans up and they can hear the difference. Of course, if you gate the drums very tightly this is not something you need to worry about (although you can open a Pandora's Box of other worries).

The problem is that many drummers like a very loosely gated drum kit and all sorts of rings can develop between drums. Most drum techs and drummers are good tuners of their kits, so more often than not the drum pitches are right where they need to be before you ever turn them up in the PA. Some rooms can present problems though, and it's those days you need to ask the drum tech for a little love.

8/20/93 Van Halen

Drum techs whose job it is to prepare the drum kit for the musician every day, as well as drummers themselves, will discover with time the best pitches to tune their drums in order to achieve the best results. Some of the results they are striving for are consistent pitch, a drum that stays in tune throughout the show, and drum heads that are at the proper tension to work most effectively for playability. This is about as deep into the world of percussion as I care to go.

What's good for the drum on stage is usually what is best for the drum sound once it's miked up and brought through the PA system. Good drum tuners will find the most correct resonant frequency of the drum and they can usually get it right around the same pitch every time. What is required of the soundman is to let the resonant pitch of the drum work for you and not against you. We all like to get that big cannon-like drum sound, unless the style of music does not call for that. I have found the best approach to achieving this is accentuating what the drum is giving you.

I've often caught myself, especially with a limited soundcheck, needing more bottom end on a tom and simply reaching up and grabbing the low-end knob on the channel EQ (without looking to see what frequency I'm boosting) and boosting 6 dB. This often gives an immediate sense of fullness to the tom and temporarily works. What I'm suggesting takes a little more time, so if you don't have more than a couple of minutes of soundcheck, you might want to save this for another time.

The process goes like this: Boost the low end on the tom 6 to 9 dB (first, turn down the overall level of the drum), and then with a narrow bandwidth sweep through the low-end frequencies until you find the frequency where the resonant pitch of the drum seems to be. If you accentuate *this* frequency a little instead of just boosting low end at any frequency you will find that the tom will probably sing a little more. By doing this to all the tom-toms as well as the snare and kick drum, you will find that you have a much more musical sounding kit, as opposed to a kit that just seems to have low end and high end, and scattered drum tones that run together.

This doesn't always work if the resonant pitch of the tom you are trying to boost is the same pitch as a dominant frequency in the room. It can just be too much. Sometimes you have to go fishing for a more suitable frequency to boost for that room. As always, do what sounds best and keep in mind that sometimes the resonant pitch of a tom might be higher than you would think. Boosting somewhere near 200 Hz on a small rack tom gives a much more musical sounding effect than trying to push air lower than that. Another good reason for doing this is if the room seems to get muddy come show time. You may need to roll off some low end on the drums and boost a little high end to get them to cut through, and you will already have the frequency selected that will help you get the most out of the low-end cut you're trying to make.

"PUT YOUR SOUNDCHECK TO TAPE"

There are lots of ways to check and tune your PA every day. The standard methods include tuning with a CD or DAT, or speaking into a mic and using your voice as a reference. Here is another method that has helped with tuning the sound system and also helped to serve as test program for other purposes. The first thing you need is a DAT, Minidisc, or other digital recording device that you can record to. What you want to do is record sounds that you usually check with band technicians or musicians available, such as drums, kick, snare and toms preferably, and also bass guitar. These first few examples are beneficial for giving you a more real reference for checking the low end of the room and not relying on a tuning song that may have unrealistic compressed bottom end on it.

By being able to hear the drum kit and bass guitar hours before they are usually set up on stage, and using these credible sounds to aid in setting up your low-end EQ is a real plus. Having drum sounds on tape is also very helpful in the programming of effects for various songs. When you first start a tour with a band, or when a new record comes out, the band will often ask you to duplicate the reverbs and delays that were used on the recording. This is tough to do when the band is around, because your attention is usually somewhere else when the drummer is hitting his drums. For this reason, having his drum kit on tape to play over and over while searching for that perfect snare reverb is a blessing.

This also allows you to avoid having to ask the drum tech to hit a snare drum for ten minutes straight while you spin parameters in your digital reverb device. A suggestion for the design of the tape could be as follows: Record two or three minutes of the snare, kick, and toms, one at a time, for the effects set up purpose, and then have the drum tech (or better; the drummer himself) play a little straight time, and record this for checking the PA. This could hold true for all the instruments you might want to work with extensively. Another handy thing to have on tape is a "click" of some kind to aid in setting up accurate delay times. This works pretty well when you don't have a computer with a delay find program around. When you listen to a very short snap or crack you can help yourself identify if the delay time between two sets of speakers is confirming the math you did to select your delay time.

You might also want to have a couple minutes of pink noise and several different tones (100 Hz and 1 kHz etc.) to assist you when the console you are using does not come equipped with a noise generator. Make a tape like this and carry it to every soundcheck and production rehearsal. The time saved can be used for other things, and the band techs will think you're a hero for saving their time as well. Remember that for general use, anyone's drum kit will be beneficial, but if you are getting ready to do a long tour with a new act, recording their actual instruments is a more accurate reference from which to draw test data. Ok, quiet on the set and roll tape!

"I DON'T NEED NO STINKING SOUNDCHECK"

A lot of times we are faced with the situation of being the opening act mixer and rarely, if ever, getting a full soundcheck through the PA. On one tour that I did a few years ago, this was the situation. We did about twenty shows with a major touring act, and as the opening act, our soundcheck privileges were non-existent. We had to wait for the headliner to do their soundcheck before we could set up for ours, as is customary, but there always seemed to be some kind of delay in their band's arrival to the venue. Even though we were instructed at the beginning of our stint that we could never make any noise through the PA once the doors were open, it turned out that from first show to the very last, I never got to hear an instrument or vocal mic through the PA before the show.

This is a rather challenging situation. For one, the drummer had seven roto-toms instead of regular toms, so the tuning and gating duties without hearing them through the PA were real tough. I was forced to listen to the instruments in a set of headphones every day and hope for the best when the show started. It really becomes a challenge when you aren't the one EQ'ing the PA. I would try to arrive before the PA tuning would take place so I could walk around and get a feel for the sound of the room and the coverage. One lesson here is to avoid expecting the sound you hear from the PA and room to resemble what you hear clearly in your headphones at line check. When you get a normal soundcheck, you tend to just check the line in the headphones and then EQ the instrument through the PA. When you are in a headphones only situation, the tendency is to hear that instrument a little more closely in your cans and then fight a little disappointment when the show starts and everything is a little rough.

Do your normal check every day but treat the show like it's the beginning. As soon as the band starts playing, dive in and sort things out as fast as you can. Don't be discouraged if things are a little out of whack. Just mix by instinct and make whatever adjustments you feel are necessary right then. It's a whole different world when you aren't combining *your* PA tuning with the way you have your board EQ set. Don't second-guess yourself or the tuning of the PA or any pre-EQ choices you may have made in the headphones. Just change whatever needs to be changed to make it right. The best revenge for not being given a soundcheck is pulling off a great sounding show and making the headline band's mixer sweat a little, soundcheck or not.

"KICK OPEN THE GATES"

2/18/95 Van Halen

Effectively using signal processing gear such as compressors and gates is important in controlling your mix. One recommendation that I have for gating kick drums has a tie-in with using two mics on the kick drum. I've spoke about the two-mic system with kick drums elsewhere. This process helps to keep the kick drum sounding tight and allows the attack to cut through while keeping the low end under control. I like to use one mic to pick up the attack of the drum and also the punch of the upper lows, and the second mic to take care of just the lower subby frequencies.

By letting the gate open easier on the attack mic while staying closed until the drum is hit harder on the subby mic, a number of benefits arise. First, many drummers complain that they listen to a board tape and don't hear all the kick drum beats coming through on tape. This can often happen if the drummer just isn't hitting the drum hard enough and it's getting lost in the mix, or it can be our fault if we have the gate set too tight on the kick channel. For this reason I like to have the gate set looser one the attack mic so that the attack of the drum comes through even if the drum is not hit really hard. One fact of acoustic and amplified drum sounds is that if a drum is not hit really hard, it will tend to have a more round and bottomy sound whereas a firmly struck drum will tend to be brighter and a little less full in the lower frequencies.

With this is mind, keeping the subby kick mic closed via the gate if the drum is not hit very hard works to your advantage. Only the mic that is taking care of the attack and upper low frequencies will come through and instead of having a droning subby sound on a light hit, you'll only have the upper lows come through, giving you a tighter kick sound. When the kick drum is struck firmly, the subby kick mic gate opens and the low end needed comes through. If you try this out you will probably agree you get a better, tighter sounding kick drum.

"OPEN THE GATE AND KEEP THE FEEDBACK OUT"

7/16/94 Ted Nugent

Signal processing equipment such as noise gates and compressors are wonderful tools of the trade, but like all things that are intended to make our lives a little better, there is a natural tendency to overuse them. A noise gate is a great device to help tailor the decay time of drums and keep unwanted cymbal splash and extraneous noise out of microphones on toms and other drums. The problems can start when we look at a noise gate on a badly tuned tom or kick drum as the fix-all to our problems. If a drum is tuned badly it will probably sound bad whether it is gated or not. I will admit that a reasonably tight noise gate on a drum channel has provided a quick fix for me before when I have been faced with little or no soundcheck and the drums are hopelessly out of tune.

The obvious—but not always possible—solution is to get the drums tuned as well as possible and then use the noise gate, if it is needed at all, to control the decay time of the drum. This is not always an option, so if you are forced to use a noise gate to help get a little more punch out of your drum sound, be sure to be aware of what would be occurring if the noise gate was bypassed. If the only way to get a floor tom to sound good is to gate it very tightly and then turn it way up, be conscious that if that noise gate was to open for very long, you could run into droning feedback problems. A good test of this is to try to get the most out of a drum's sound with the noise gate in bypass mode. Then when you think you have done all you can, engage the gate and see if that cleans up the tone a little. Try to use long release times and gentle thresholds, unless you are going for a quick gated sound as an effect. When you think you have things where you are happy, try bypassing the gate and see if the drum goes wildly into feedback when it or another drum is hit. If this is the case, you will probably be forced to turn the overall level of that drum down.

It is true that with noise gates it is often possible to get considerably more gain out of a drum because the after ring is controlled, but don't fall into the trap of over-gating and boosting gain everywhere. What will often happen is that when the drummer goes into a fury of double bass drums at warp speed, all your tom channel gates will open at once and wild feedback will ensue. Try instead to get all the reasonable level you can out of your drum channels without gates, and then put your gates in line to tidy up the over-rings.

9/16/94 Jon Secada

Noise gates can be valuable tools for trying to control ringing and leakage in individual drum channels. As with any product, there are some gates that just seem to work a little better than others. Certain gates can make an audible 'tick' sound as they open and close if the threshold, attack and release times are set a little too tight. Other gates let you get away with a little tighter setting. I personally prefer to have a noise gate work as naturally as possible in most situations, unless you are trying to go for an accentuated "gate" effect. By naturally, I mean a nice smooth attack and release time, so that the gate opens and closes naturally, the way a tom-tom will decay after it is hit. This will help to keep that annoying 'tick' sound from occurring as well.

If you're having trouble with the bleed from other drums opening your gates, try utilizing the key filter option if your gate has this feature. What this set of parameters allows you to do is zero in on a frequency, and an adjustable bandwidth around that frequency. This is what the gate will open to. In essence, the frequency you select is what the gate is "listening" for, and this triggers it to open. Key filtering, when used efficiently, is a tool that will allow you to raise the threshold of gating so that your gate will stay closed to more outside bleed. All of this will give you a nice loose gate to give the drum you are gating a more natural sound, and yet still keep the gate closed to outside noise (and inside noise like those nasty 'ticks'). Don't run to the drug store to solve your tick problem, just work with your gates a little. (See "Trigger happy," page 22 for more gating tricks.)

CHAPTER 15

Effects and Signal Processing

As we think back over the years to the songs that made an impact on us, the ones that really made us feel something, it's very likely there was a mood set by reverb or another kind of special effect used brilliantly. Who can forget the depth of emotion that was created in "Unchained Melody" by the Righteous Brothers or the wide range of effects used to mix "In the Air Tonight" by Phil Collins? These studio masterpieces have sent live sound engineers racing to the audio mags to fill out their Christmas wish lists for their upcoming tours while sound company vendors figure out how they're going to recoup the money they must spend purchasing that one vintage tube compressor. It can become a bit of a game. I admit high-end gear is wonderful to work with, and lengthy, moneymaking tours deserve the fine gear their engineers request, but when you're playing the "Enormodome," the margin of difference between a standard reverb device and an elaborate device is minimal. What really makes the difference most of the time is execution. Using that reverb or delay just the way the album used it, or fine-tuning the drums with precise gating are the variables that make the most impact on your mix.

Like everything else in life, it starts with some basics. Paying attention to gain structure when using a compressor, for example, will make or break the outcome of the object you're effecting. There's a little bit of "Signal processing 101" to follow, but hang in there, I never take you back to the classroom for very long.

"YOU DON'T GET NOTHIN' FOR FREE"

4/28/93 Van Halen

It's very easy when using compression on vocals to think that you're getting some free gain along the way. "If I compress this vocal a little more and then turn up the gain, I'll have a louder vocal...right? Without those pesky too quiet and too loud parts...right?" Well the truth of the matter is, by knocking back the loudest parts of the singer's level and turning up the compressor output gain a bit you will indeed get a little extra overall gain. Just remember that the boosted output gain on the compressor is a boost in level whether there is any input into it or not.

What I'm getting at is potential problems relating to level before feedback. If you get a singer's mic tuned and EQ'd and you find that pushing the fader to +5 dB on his channel starts to get you into feedback problems, then be wary if you start to go for extra gain from the compressor output. If you increase the compressor output to +5 dB, you have essentially brought the channel fader's threshold of feedback down from +5 dB to 0 dB. This problem happens a lot when you have a singer who whispers a bunch and then screams very loudly at other times. You find that you have to compress those very loud parts quite a bit, and when you see that you're compressing 6 or 8 dB of level, you try to get a little back at the output of the compressor for those whispery parts. This is fine as long as you don't try to get too much back and get yourself into feedback potential. The problem will occur when the vocal is not being compressed at all. This is when that 5 dB of gain that you added at the output stage of the compressor is added to whatever level you have set at the channel input gain stage, plus the fader level.

To test your true level before feedback, always be sure you are ringing out a mic with the compressor in line so that its boosted gain is part of the gain structure you're EQ'ing with. If the mic can sit on a stand with no compression occurring and still be ring free, then you're doing great. This problem occurs most often when you're doing a one-off and you haven't got the time to do a thorough EQ'ing job. If you get a five second soundcheck on the vocals you're happy. So when the show starts you start inserting compressors and doing a little of the aforementioned gain boosting.

Be aware that if the vocal starts to feedback halfway through a show when it was fine at the beginning, a good place the look for the cause of the problem is your compressor gain staging. If you really need a couple of extra dB of gain to have that vocal cut through, try increasing the threshold of your compressor so you're not compressing quite as much. Then work the manual-fader compressor a little more. What's that? You say. Oh, that's the process of using your finger to move the vocalist's fader up and down to control volume; a novel approach.

"PAY ATTENTION TO YOUR GOZINTAS AND GOZOUTAS!"

5/1/93 Van Halen

When you need more effects in your mix, be sure to think carefully about where you are going to get that extra level. It's easy to just reach for the effects send on the channel, or the overall auxiliary output send, but be careful that you don't overload the input to the reverb or delay unit. A lot of the gear we use these days passes much of the signal in the digital domain. When you clip the input to a digital device the resulting return signal can be quite ugly. This is especially true with digital effects processors. With the myriad of effects out there, from chorus and long delays to harmonizing and pitch changes, the amount of processing involved is quite intense within the circuitry of the unit. If you begin this process with an overloaded signal, the return can really sound nasty.

If you need more overall effects return, you should first check that you are sending enough signal to the unit, so that you're not trying to process a bunch of hiss, which sounds equally as heinous as overloading the input. You can then get the extra return level at the channel input gains on the console where you have the effect returning. You will be able to get that effect loud and ominous (and clean too) if you just follow the golden gain structure rule: correct level in, and adjust for necessary return gain at the point where the effect returns to the console. Be sure to check these levels periodically if you're on a long tour as you can go through many gain structure changes and these ups and downs in channel gain will affect your effects in and out levels.

Most of today's effects gear has clearly identifiable input metering (green, yellow, and red), so the task at hand is to find the input level that hangs around the 0 dB mark, only occasionally tickling +3 dB or so. If the gain structure on the rest of your board is consistent and you haven't over EQ'd anything drastically, you should have a nice clean result. Then, when the artist asks for eight seconds of reverb on his voice, you can deliver it with pristine clarity.

"PHASEY LIKE A FOX"

6/23/93 Van Halen

One of the sinister threats to good sound is phasing problems. It's a drag to find you've been EQ'ing and chasing your tail trying to discover why something (that is, two or more channels of something) doesn't sound quite right, and then you reverse the phase on one of the two channels and find everything sounds like it should. Always be aware of this potential problem. The golden rule to remember is: Always be checking for it. It's tougher to do if you don't have phase reverse buttons on the channels of your mixing board. If you do though, and you're dealing with two stereo lines of keyboards, or more than one source sound like bass DI and mic, snare top and bottom, put one out of phase and see what happens.

If you don't have phase reverse buttons on your console, always have a phase reverse cable ready to insert in your console's channel input if you suspect you have a problem. The telltale sign of things being out of phase is low-end decrease when the second channel is turned up. For example, if you're checking the bass and you're listening to just the DI sound and then you add the bass mic channel to it, you can suspect there's a problem if there is more bottom with just the one channel than with both turned on. Obviously, the best time to check this is when you are dialing up a mix for the first time. If you are going from console to console with the same band from day to day, using different mics and mic cables, the potential for a problem goes way up. Check this every day even if things start out sounding OK. You will catch yourself thinking things were fine and then find out they weren't in phase when you pop in that old button.

Beware of things like changed speakers within a guitar cabinet as well. Sometimes backline guys make a mistake and wire a replaced speaker out of phase, and you can be the one to catch this if the now thin-sounding guitar rig gets magically better in your headphones or PA with a flipped phase button. You can then saunter up to the guitar tech and advise him of his problem. If you do it out of earshot of the guitar player he'll probably buy you a cocktail later. If you use the same rig every day with the same brand gear, you may just remind yourself to do a periodic phasing maintenance check. You never know what might happen with people rooting around the innards of keyboard racks. Definitely have a check if something that usually sounded solid starts sounding thin.

"WHAT GOES IN MUST COME OUT"

8/5/96 Gin Blossoms

Compressors are very handy tools that make your overall gain structure work much more smoothly. Using a compressor incorrectly, however, can cause serious problems. Always be aware of what you are trying to achieve by compressing the instrument, vocal, or mix in question. When you use a compressor on a vocal there is a tendency to make to compressor function as the never-ending gain booster. We've all done it to some extent, at least early on in our careers.

The problems start when you begin turning the gain up too much at the input or output stage of the compressor. I'm sure you've encountered the scenario where you need a little more level on the lead vocal mic and so you reach up to the input attenuation knob on the channel and give it a click or two more. That doesn't seem to do the trick and so you reach up for a dB or two more. That still doesn't seem to be enough, and so you go for more. I think you get the picture.

Have you figured out the problem yet? If you have a compressor across the channel, the more you increase the gain going into the compressor the more the signal is compressed. If you look down at this point you will probably notice that you are hitting well into compression and that darn vocal just isn't gettin' any louder. The trick to getting a little more gain is to use the output gain control of the compressor. You first want to turn the input attenuation down a bit so that you aren't hitting into so much compression, and then give yourself that extra little bit of gain at the output of the compressor.

This comes with a warning. If you were to remove the compressor from the link you would find that turning the input attenuation on the channel up and up would eventually cause you to clip the input of the channel. The same holds true with the compressor in line. By turning up the output gain control of the compressor you will find that the input level (as seen by your channel LED or PFL when cued up) will continue to rise as you turn up this level. This is not free gain. The message here again brings us to overall gain structure. You must have the correct relationship between channel-input gain, group output and master output level. The compressor will help you achieve an overall better consistency of level. And if more level is what you're after, you can get it by giving a slight nudge at the output knob.

To ensure you're not cheating, though, give yourself the following little test periodically. While someone is speaking into the microphone (or playing the instrument if that is the case), pop the insert button in and out to be sure that the level with or without the compressor in line is about the same. If the level is considerably louder with the compressor inserted, then you have probably boosted too much output on the compressor and you would be better served to take the compressor out of line and readjust the channel's input attenuation. When you have things at a good loud level, you can then reinsert the compressor. (Be sure to turn the output of the compressor down a little before you reinsert the compressor, it may be screaming loud). Doing this occasionally keeps you honest and also double-checks that knobs on the compressor didn't get bumped as the gear moved from one gig to the next.

PART SIX: SHOWTIME

SHOWTIME

At least once during every tour that I've done, there would come a time when I'd need to take a stroll out to the lobby of the venue just before the start of the show to look at the people coming in. It seemed necessary to remind myself that this is a big night for them. They had been looking forward to this for some time and now the night was finally here. It was finally showtime!

When it all comes down to it, we're in the entertainment business. We facilitate our clients' need to hear their music, and have the fans hear it as well. The exciting part about all this is that we get to be in on the end result, the show. We are intimately involved in the most exhilarating part of the whole deal. We should never forget that. When things get rough, when we're in the middle of a six in a row, it's beneficial to remember that we are part of the most personal part of an artist's career: his or her songs being played for his or her fans. It's great!

Whatever obstacles may have presented themselves to you during the load-in, setup, tuning and soundcheck are all just memories now. It only paves the way to the first downbeat of the first song. Let that stuff go and have fun in the moment, even if the moment is consisting of a really bad start to a show in a really bad room. You'll pull it together; the artist is banking on it. With all the skills you've acquired and all the heart and effort you've poured in to this, it's only a matter of time (it would be great if that time was only one or two songs though…right?).

Aside from the occasional moments when a band's manager leans over my shoulder to suggest a mix tip or two, this is the time when it's all in my hands. It can be overwhelming, but it's also a great feeling to trust in your abilities and then simply get lost in the mix. It's really great when the conditions are right and it's all falling into place. The culmination of everything you've worked so hard for can sometimes be captured on those nights and you can manage a moment of nostalgia within the show to reflect on how it's all worked out so well. Enjoy it.

The notes to follow run the gamut of mixing a rock or pop show. There are many facets of this, as you'll see. We'll touch on a bunch of them and you'll probably be ready to crash in your bunk on the bus by the time we're done, just as if you mixed a real show.

CHAPTER 16

Before the Lights Go Out

If your front-of-house area right before showtime resembles Cape Canaveral just prior to a shuttle launch then you're going to feel like I'm preaching to the choir in this section. If you're the kind that kicks back with a latte just before the lights go down and mumbles casually, "It all worked in soundcheck so it should be fine now," these notes to follow are prepared with you in mind!

We're going to have a little heart-to-heart about pre-show preparation. Remember as you read each one of the following notes that they came from the school of hard knocks. We will revisit some of the mistakes I've made in the first song or two, and some suggestion will be passed on to you now to hopefully steer you clear of the dangers in the future.

Preparation, preparation, preparation. One more time: preparation. That's all you really need to avoid early show fatalities. Read on to learn every sordid detail.

"READY, SET, GO!"

11/17/99 Luis Miguel

Ok, this is a short one, and this tip is so simple and fundamental that we often forget to do this. You've done a soundcheck earlier in the day, and if you have an opening act, you've probably just concluded a second line check prior to your band hitting the stage. They hit the first downbeat of the first song. Is everything working? Is everything coming up as it should in the correct channels? Is each channel's corresponding gate or compressor working correctly? These should be checked right away.

If you're doing a lot of one-offs, you probably fall right into this habit once you've spun up something resembling a band mix with a vocal on top. This should always be the first priority. Get some semblance of a mix going and then do some mental checks. Just the other night I was doing an arena that had an unusually thick sub slap that really masked the definition down low. I noticed that after about three songs I was missing something. Well (I'm blushing here), it was my bass guitar.

It's easy to sit back and say, "How do you miss an entire instrument?" But if you've done any arena mixing you will know that many rooms are very thick in the sub-bass area and the bass guitar tends to get washed out a lot. I mistook the washy low end for my inability to define the bass, when the actual problem was that the output knob on the bass compressor had been bumped. This resulted in a –10db output level coming from the compressor. I turned it up and things came together in the mix, and it was at that moment that I cursed myself and decided to write this down. It's perspiration and inspiration all at the same time.

The method I would suggest is to immediately follow the 'getting the mix together' thing with a quick blast up the input channel PFL highway. Start at the first channel and have a quick listen and then move on. This might not be as convenient as listening to the groups and then moving on, but you might miss something that way. As I've suggested in another memo, having a pre-show checklist will help you catch these little moved knob situations, but a quick once-over at the beginning of the show will confirm everything is there. It's that simple.

"DARTH VADER YOU DON'T NEED"

8/28/97 Engelbert Humperdinck

Effects can take an average show and add all the glitz and sparkle that make a great show. If you have a nice, acoustically dead environment to mix in your choice of effects can make or break your mix. One of the bad habits I've found myself getting into over the years is checking effects returns during the day and then assuming the parameters are not going to change at all before the show. You can be pretty sure that all is OK with most effects units because you physically have to call up edit parameter pages to get in there and muck around with things, but some units have parameter adjustment wheels on the front, and they have been known to get bumped here and there which can cause some embarrassing moments.

One unit in particular that I am speaking of is a certain kind of harmonizer. It has a spinning wheel on the front panel that is very easy to turn, and on one occasion I just happened to catch myself before I made a horrendous mistake. The last thing that I was editing that afternoon was the pitch of the harmonizer. Without changing that edit page, the wheel got bumped later on in the day and just before showtime I happened to listen to my effects returns and catch the mistake before the show started. If I had not, the two lovely ladies who were singing backup vocals for the show would have resembled Darth Vader much more than their normal sweet-sounding southern selves. The edit wheel had spun down and the pitch dropped considerably.

Another way that you can get caught is if someone, like an opening act engineer, makes adjustments to your effects during his show and forgets to tell you, or you forget to recall your program or parameters. Usually these days most opening acts get their own effects gear, but in many club situations everybody is sharing effects. Be sure to store your settings, and in those types of situations, double check that nothing is out of whack. It's a good habit to get into. Unfortunately, aside from the benefit that all these programmable units have given us, they can catch us once in a while because we rely too much on their stability. Add this to your pre show checklist. And use the force!

"PRE-SHOW CHECK 1, CHECK 2"

7/15/90 Aerosmith

There's nothing quite as embarrassing as flying out of the gate at the start of the show with something not working. Or the always-exciting pad getting kicked out on the lead vocal channel and howling feedback greeting the enthusiastic throng. Not only do you feel like an idiot, you also get to think about your goof for the entire show.

A good way to combat this kind of catastrophe is to have a pre-show checklist. I like to put it on the first page of my show notes so that as I get ready to mix I have a visual reminder of some basic check points to pay attention to. Some of these checks may include looking to see that your effects are on the right program, or that your EQ has not been bumped during the after-soundcheck hours before the show. Some other checkpoints could be a gain level and pad check on your channels.

I know you may feel like you have just done a soundcheck so you should be fine, but certain situations like a rowdy club or an outdoor show where you're removing weather coverings like plastic or space blankets can accidentally cause a knob to move. I write this memo after having made a rather large goof the other night. After cleaning the board with a wet paintbrush, one of my reverb returns got un-assigned from the stereo bus, and I started out with no reverb on the lead vocal, a very important element of this artist's sound. Some bands, like the one I'm mixing right now, don't soundcheck, and therefore your chance for a first song botch is much higher. If you run MIDI in your rig you might want to check that your MIDI program changes are actually happening.

Things like gates and compressor knobs can also get bumped during setup and you might not necessarily catch that during the soundcheck. This is a good time to ensure you have the correct song list for the show and if you are lucky to be running an automated board like the AMEK Recall, you will want to ensure your song list is in the same order. Other things might include checking to see that you have a fresh tape in the tape deck for recording and that all of your possible playback cues (on DAT or CD) are cued up to the right spot and ready to go in order. If you are doing a show in the middle of the day outside, you will want to be extra careful to check that all of your devices are powered up and working correctly, because the sunlight can make it real hard to see things work. You will definitely find the list that works for you, and you may find that after making a mistake during a show you will want to add something to your list to catch this problem before it can happen again. The best result that will be achieved is a calm and confident you getting behind the mixing board, knowing that all is in order and as it should be. All you have to do now is mix and think about the way your rig sounds. Get a checkup before the show to ensure healthy audio for you and all your adoring fans.

"DON'T SHOUT BEFORE YOU SPEAK"

5/23/95 Van Halen

The lights go down. The dry ice creeps over the front of the stage. The crowd is frantic as a low rumble builds and builds until the ceiling tiles are falling out of the roof and people are ready to run from the building. Just as you think you can't take it any more, the rumble builds to a deafening, throbbing crescendo and then is abruptly cut off by blinding light and a band on stage that sounds as if it is playing through a transistor radio.

Sound familiar? Hey, it has happened to me. The darned intro tape can kill you every time. And why is it that bands always want to use something that has 4 Hz in it to open the show? Go figure.

The problem that causes this discrepancy in level is usually SPL reference. During the afternoon when you soundchecked the band in an empty room the volume of the intro tape seemed quite substantial. But after an opening act and the roar of the audience as the house lights go off, you find yourself pushing the level of that intro tape higher and higher, leaving the band to come out sounding less than impressive.

You need to establish the maximum level that the intro "rumble" DAT can go before it upstages your band's first song power level, and not be freaked out if it doesn't sound loud enough as it's rolling. It's better to start out with the intro sounding a bit low and the band sounding a little loud than the other way around. I refuse to let all the frequency bands through when this type of tape is handed to me. If the bottom end of the band doesn't usually live in the 30-40 Hz region for most of the show, then I'm going to high-pass my DAT intro tape to at least 40 or 50 Hz.

You want the audience to remember the first note the band plays with an overwhelmed feeling, so let it be good and powerful. Don't let a silly tape that was produced and mixed at

Skywalker Ranch give your sub-bass speakers too much of a workout before the real deal comes on stage. Save the best for last and lighten up on intro overload.

"STOP THE BLEEDING"

5/26/94 Extreme

This is one of those things that hopefully only happens to you once in your audio lifetime, and if it does happen, you hope that it does so during a soundcheck and not during the show. To communicate to the stage throughout the day, and to speak to the artist during soundcheck, we set up a 'talkback' mic that is routed through the snake to the monitor board so that the front-of-house guy can have his voice magically appear in the monitors on stage. This useful process can considerably extend the life of a front-of-house mixer's vocal cords, as he or she doesn't have to yell 100 feet to the stage all day long.

The danger of having this mic is that if you happen to leave it on while you have the PA roaring away, there will be a ton of bleed back to the monitors and the monitor guy will begin pulling his hair out trying to find the root of the problem. This really is more of a warning to the monitor engineers out there, but the fault lies with the front-of-house mixer. We all hate having our talkback mics shut off by the monitor guy because we are then forced to scream loud enough for someone to turn it back on. Therefore, we must be responsible enough to turn our talkback mics off out front so that the monitor guy can safely leave it turned on up there on stage.

The simplest solution is to get a mic with an on/off switch and always have it in the off position when you aren't speaking to the stage. One simple rule of thumb that ensures that the show will not have this problem is unplugging the talkback completely from the mic cable before the show starts. The monitor guy should always have the talkback channel muted once the show begins, but this is an extra safety measure to ensure the front-of-house mix does not find its way back on stage.

CHAPTER 17

In the Heat of Battle

Swords are drawn, negotiations are over, and the battle flags have been raised...It's showtime! It's you versus the room. Charge!

This is the fastest ten minutes of your day, without a doubt. You may find yourself needing to consciously take a breath, seeing how you've been holding it for the entire last song. You'll soon settle in to the mix and gravitate towards cruise control. When you have some time to think and not just respond, hopefully you'll think a little bit about some of the notes to follow. There are some helpful hints directly related to mixing the show. All the preparations you do throughout the day are a part of how the final mix sounds, but the audience, the band, and concerned parties like the band's manager may judge your performance during these 90 minutes only. It's your time to shine. Let me show you some tidbits that have helped give my mixes some more gloss.

"THIS 'ZIZZ' A GREAT WAY TO IMPROVE YOUR VOCAL SOUND"

3/22/96 Julio Iglesias

Sometimes it seems you've done all you can to clean up the sound of a vocal and it still isn't cutting through the mix. You may be bothered by a low-mid thing and so you dig that out of the EQ. Then something starts biting you in the upper mid, so you go back in with your shovel to solve that problem. It can seem that you are cutting and cutting and turning up and turning up, and the same frequencies just keep coming back to haunt you. What I've done in the past that seems to help is to add a little 'zizz' to the channel EQ, and sometimes the system EQ, to give the sound some breath. By 'zizz' I mean the really high top end stuff around 12 or 16k Hz. By adding this to your vocal channel EQ with the narrowest bandwidth on your parametric EQ, you can fabricate this whole new 'air' to the vocals without making them too sibilant or too loud. It will just help it to cut through better.

The effectiveness of this may vary, depending on the type of mic the singer is singing through and the quality of high-end drivers the system is packing. Be sure to have someone check the amplifiers for clipping, as these frequencies can put a strain on your high-end drivers. Remember, these tips don't always work in every situation, but I can confidently say that I've managed to add life to some pretty lifeless PAs by smoothing out the high-mid bite, and then adding some breath to the top end response of the system. Give it a try and remember that medicine is best taken in small doses at first. Try a little and see what happens. This 'zizzn't' going to let you down.

"IT'LL ALL PAN OUT"

10/12/94 Jon Secada

There will be times when you'll find you have to battle the gain-before-feedback problem with a roving lead vocalist mic. You may have tuned the PA and rung out the mic to achieve maximum gain during the day, but the noise of a boisterous crowd and ripping guitars is leaving your vocal level a touch shy in the mix. As you reach for a little more vocal gain you may start to hear the howls and screeches of feedback as it invades your cozy world.

You may also notice as the singer goes to the downstage corners of the stage and puts himself and the mic in front of the PA that this problem becomes worse. The only thing I can suggest for the problem of feedback is to try and grab the worst frequencies that are ringing and pull them back a bit or bring back the overall mix volume respectively. As for the singer moving out into the combat zone, I have a little tip that seems to help, even though it may be a slight bit of a cheat. If your system is in stereo, you can reach for the pan knob on the singer's vocal mic channel as he goes for that downstage corner. If he is heading in front of your house left stack, pan his vocal slightly to the right in the mix. If you go too far, you may notice that it starts sounding a touch weird, but a slight pan (not much more than say 2 o'clock) should suffice in keeping the vocal level up in the PA, while keeping the squeaks down.

If you are sitting in the crowd in the left hand side of the house, you will probably hear the vocal fade away a bit, but you would have heard that anyway if you merely brought the vocal fader down to keep it below feedback. If you are sitting in the house right zone, you will hear the same abundant level of vocal out of the house right stack, and you will probably not notice that tricks are being played on you. It's a game of playing the odds and giving a larger percentage of the house the correct level of vocal while keeping the feedback under wraps.

The best solution is always going to be using your arsenal of tricks to tune the sound system correctly and efficiently to avoid feedback in the first place, but when you need that "extra little push over the cliff," reach for the pan knob and moonwalk your vocalist's mic over to the other side of the stage. Everyone will appreciate it and maybe your raise will pan out as well.

"KNOCKOUT PUNCH"

2/13/95 Van Halen

I think if we asked drummers whether they mind if the noise gates on their drums don't quite open all the way all the time, I'm pretty sure we would get a similar answer from most of them: "Yes, I mind."

The problem we, in the audio business, deal with on a daily basis is how to have the noise gates effectively keep things out of the mics, especially the tom mics, and also control the decay of the drums, while still allowing the lightest of hits to make it through. Anyone reading this who has struggled as much as I have will wholeheartedly agree that this is tough. I have found that several tricks will help, but the name of the game really is compromise. There has to be some give and take with the drummer and sound engineer. Either the noise gates are tight enough to keep out the noise, cymbals and hi-hats, or they are very loose and only there to keep mics closed between songs. This is often the harsh reality of the situation.

One way to compromise that has worked well for me is to pick your spots. By this I mean that there are times when you can punch out the noise gates to ensure that nothing gets cut off, and then punch them back in when things get rockin' again. An example of this is punching out the insert button on the tom channels during a drum solo. Now, I know the days of big flashy drum solos are mostly behind us, but some big rock bands and jazz drummers still like to strut their stuff. When the drummer gets the board tape at the end of the night, he may go directly to the drum solo to hear how he performed. It is a good thing if his paradiddles and flams are all there and not being gobbled up by fickle noise gates.

Always be sure to have the tones and rings of the drums controlled before inserting noise gates in the chain during soundcheck. If you punch out the gates during a drum solo and the world starts rolling and feeding back in the low end, you are not going to look so good. Some songs have quiet intros or breaks where the drummer may do some light work on the drums; here is another place where you can punch out those gates and ensure all is well. During most of the show, if the drummer hits quite hard, you can be pretty safe with your regular gate threshold settings, but you may find they are too tight for a delicate piece of music. Compromise, give the drummer his moments, and he will probably be much more willing to let a tightly gated drum kit pass inspection if it helps the overall sound.

"GIVE YOUR SINGER A PLACE TO LIVE"

6/14/94 Extreme

I can't say enough about the importance of starting a show with and maintaining a standard of keeping the lead vocalist on top of the mix when it comes to most pop/rock acts that we go to see live. There is a big problem with this in our industry, and it can be really frustrating for the audience as they try to sing along or merely understand what the singer is singing. Two problems that contribute to this are a poorly EQ'd lead vocal, and as I've discussed elsewhere, starting the show with too many effects muddying up the mix.

One thing that I do at the start of the show that helps to give the lead vocal a place in the mix is to start with the cymbals turned down somewhat. This clears up the high end initially so that the lead vocal presence can punch through. I group the hi-hat, ride, and crash cymbals together on a group or VCA so that I can easily bring down the overall level of all the cymbals at the start of the show. Also, you can try to clean up any bitey or piercing upper frequencies on the guitars, or any other instruments that tend to get in the singer's way. If this seems like an unfair compromise in favor of the singer, keep in mind that this only needs to be a temporary thing. Once you have established level and clarity on the main vocal you can sneak things back into the mix to polish up what you have going.

The main principle here is to start with a crisp, clean lead vocal, establish its place on top of the mix, and then build the fullness and sweetness of the other instruments slowly and surely. If the artist you are mixing is mainly a piano or guitar player, and vocals are secondary, then I say concentrate on that instrument first. Make the thing the people came to see special and dominant and build around that. In many touring pop/rock acts the singer is not always the only star of the band and shouldn't necessarily be given all the attention in your mixing endeavors, but it is quite common that the vocal and lyrics are the most important part of the show and should be audible and crisp from the get-go. You may not want the singer living with you between gigs, but when the show begins, do the right thing.

"FILL IN THE BLANKS"

7/23/99 Luis Miguel

Be the mix, Danny. Be your future, make your future. (There's one for all you *Caddyshack* fans out there.)

Anyway, what I'm trying to say is that you are the mixer. You are the one controlling what's going on, so mix! Don't just sit or stand there. I see and hear mixers who get a type of "mix fright," where they stand frozen over the console and forget to move and participate in the music. We are involved in a technical process by which we take instruments and emotional music and turn them into analog and digital information, and then we amplify and process this musical info and spew it back out of a bunch of black lumber. Somewhere in that process we must try to feel the emotion of the music that is being played.

I find that one way to move with the music is to use breaks in the musical structure of the song to accent parts of the mix. For example, the band I'm mixing now has a horn section. If I want the horns accented while the singer is singing the verse, I'll wait until he finishes a line of vocal and then bump up the horns for a quick moment. Songs are usually structured this way so blasts of horns usually have open spaces between vocal lines to be accented. What I'm saying is, give the Horn VCA a little push during these parts to give them a volume advantage, thus being the highlight of that moment. This might sound very simplistic and obvious, but it is not always done.

Studio recordings are usually compressed a fair bit and although you hear everything great, you don't always feel certain elements of the mix jumping out at you. In live music we seem to have the advantage of letting a good guitar solo rip, or a backgroud vocal lick kick through the mix with a little fader push. Sometimes we tend to bump up the drums, followed by the guitar and then keys, and we fall victim to the "everything louder than everything else" syndrome. The trick here is to bump up the highlighted instrument or group and then back it down so the vocal sits where it should, on top of the pile. Everyone seems to like a dynamic mix and this is one way to make that happen. It isn't for every artist.

Some may have the entire band on volume pedals and wish for his or her musicians to control the mixing and highlighting of solos and bumps. If so, then I would follow the desires of my boss and let the band take care of this. You will find though, that many rooms that are very reverberant will de-emphasize the volume changes (the rising and falling of levels). Because things are being lost in the room's reverberation, you may find that you have to move a fader more to notice a difference in its volume. Again, you will be put in the position of controlling the mix more. Whatever the situation, take heart and dig in. You have been hired to mix, so be artistic and let the mix move and swing; let it come to life. Their lives are in your hands, so wait for a blank spot in the mix and fill it in.

"A LITTLE DIP 'LL DO YA"

6/26/96 Gin Blossoms

Here's a little move that you will probably find yourself doing instinctively after a short time mixing. So many artists demand monitor levels that live right on the edge of feedback, and this often becomes a problem in the house as well. To make matters worse, the singer is barely breathing into the mic and you have a big old pile of lumber (speaker boxes) within 30 feet. Sometimes these are just the facts of life in audio world, and particularly rough shows will find you chasing little feedback squeaks throughout the night.

One little trick that might help is to try to break the feedback loop before it really takes off. If you mix like I do, you always have one finger on the lead vocal fader to adjust for peaks and valleys in level that the compressor just isn't catching. With this is mind, having your attention centered on the lead vocal fader will help you stop that feedback before it starts. If you hear a frequency or two getting ready to take off, try giving the vocal fader a quick jerk down and see if that kills the impending feedback. This might not always work if the monitor guy is not following the same move you're making. If the two of you are on the same page and you are both hearing that squeak developing, a little dip on the fader will usually kill the feedback before it gets going. This may sound weird if the singer is in the middle of a vocal passage so I'll always try to time the move to occur between lines of the song or during a breath. As soon as I do the quick little move I return the vocal to the same level it was "pre-squeak" and carry on as before. It's a habitual move, and that goes to show you that it must be something that works if I've learned to do it without thinking about it. Hop on your board and ride the wave.

"WHAT DID SHE SAY?"

10/10/94 Jon Secada

How many times have you gone to see a concert or club show, and as the band starts and the music comes roaring to life, the singer steps up to sing his or her opening line and you can't hear a word that's being sung? To all the sound mixers out there, this is not an uncommon ailment and it happens to the best of us from time to time, especially if we are working with the band for the first time and do not yet know the strength of the singer's voice.

When a show opens like this we can't panic or lose faith, but merely do the obvious and sensible thing: Turn down the rest of the instruments and singers until the lead singer is firmly on top of the mix, where vocals are meant to be in most forms of modern pop and rock music. This must seem like a fairly elementary and idiotic statement to make, but getting back to my opening statement; how many times have you seen a show where there is nowhere near enough vocal level at the start of the show? To make matters worse, it doesn't improve as song after song goes by. I have witnessed mixes where the kick drum and snare reverb improve dramatically as the second song is winding down, and the guitar sound that started off rather scratchy has smoothed out, but I still can't hear the singer properly.

This is most important when the artist the paying customers are coming to see is a vocalist whose name happens to be the name on the marquee. Prepare for this as best you can during line check and soundcheck. See how much level you can get on the vocalist's mic in the PA before those good old squeaks and squawks start to creep in. If you are lucky enough to get a soundcheck with the whole band and the singer, you should use that time to get the vocal clean and clearly on top of the mix. If you don't get a soundcheck, then work on getting that vocal mic as loud as you can and note the spot on the fader, so that when the show starts you can be aware of where problems with feedback will begin.

Above all, be sure to give yourself a fighting chance at the start of the show. If you begin things with the band screaming loud, you will most likely have trouble getting the singer over that level. Start with the band at a reasonable level and once you are assured that the words the singer is singing are clear and crisp fill the mix in around that. Nothing will sink you faster with the artist than having friends and fans telling him or her that they couldn't be heard. Do the right thing: stay employed.

"IF THE SOUP'S TOO THICK, DON'T ADD FLOUR"

7/12/93 Van Halen

It's very easy to get caught up in various flavor enhancements when trying to add spice to your mix. No, this hasn't turned into a cookbook, but didn't anyone ever tell you that being a pro sound guy is a lot like being a great chef? Too many ingredients can spoil the dish.

As I've mentioned before, we are not always blessed on a day-to-day basis with the finest acoustical surroundings with which to perform our craft. When we are given one of those toilet bowl venues to mix in, I cannot stress one thing enough: the first step is to get the instruments and singers in the band as clear and defined as possible. Concern yourself more with hearing everything clearly than with having your snare reverb sounding just like the record. This is a common flaw that I see happen so much, and a very large pet peeve of mine. Very often the room you are mixing in is so thick with early reflections and reverb that the use of your pre-programmed effects is not even necessary.

I have witnessed situations where the show starts and the band is playing away with the mix all out of balance, even to the point where the drums are raging away and the singer is not even being heard. I look over at the sound guy with a "what's up?" look on my face and there he is, getting all his effects dialed in. It's true that some bands are very effects-heavy like the production of their records, and they rely somewhat on those effects to convey the songs to the audience live. The point I'm trying to make though is that some rooms won't allow you to hear the subtlety of those effects with room resonance that is so overwhelming. As always, get right to the task of getting a proper balance of everything first so the crowd can hear all the elements clearly, and then if the room allows, sneak in some effects later on to spice things up a bit. To keep the room from eating you for lunch at the start of the show, and all the way through to dessert, keep things as simple as possible until the mix settles in. Bon appetite!

2/14/91 Poison

This memo is just as valuable to the monitor engineer in the crowd but can be helpful to any mixer who has to deal with a vocalist with less-than-Herculean vocal chords. When you are dealing with a singer who sings very quietly, it is tough to use a compressor to clip off those loud bursts while getting back a little gain at the compressor gain output. Any gain added to the output of the compressor is still just gain added, so if your problem is gain before feedback, where you're not really gaining anything (pardon the pun).

If you want to use the compressor for quieting the really loud passages that's fine, but I have found in these situations that using my good old right index finger serves me just as well. I will leave the compressor in line but will use it more like a limiter with a very stiff threshold that the singer rarely hits. When he does it will jump down 8 or 10 dB in level. By keeping one finger on the vocalist's fader and riding those volume swells during the show I have had much more success than trying to set a compressor just right. I've worked with some Vegas-style artists that sing a good foot from the mic and, believe me, you need every dB of free gain you can get.

Riding those constantly changing vocal levels manually has proved much more effective than any other method. I will also bring the fader down 10 dB or so when I know the singer is between lines to eliminate the roving overhead mic syndrome. I have been caught now and then missing a prompt from the artist to the crowd to get off their seats, but that is the risk with turning the mic down during instrumental breaks and cleaning up the bleed. With some shows you are just too busy to always have one finger on the vocalist's channel, but with a show where the vocalist *is* the show and his pipes ain't what they used to be, I would incorporate the human compressor system and be your own best piece of processing gear.

6/28/96 Gin Blossoms

With some acts that we mix for, the lead vocal sound requires a very breathy, sizzling type of high end that was achieved in the studio with very expensive mics and great-sounding, high-dollar pre-amps and processing gear. These are things we live mixing guys don't get to play with much.

But all is not lost. There are a few tricks I have come across that will help with some of the problems that occur as we search for—but often have trouble getting—that airy top end on our singer's vocal. The main problems we battle are feedback of high-end frequencies, and the accentuating of high end on everything else on stage through the vocalist's mic, especially cymbals and guitar. This problem is much greater when the singer in question has very low vocal output. What works well in this case is using an expander to bring down the level of the vocal mic perhaps 10 to 15 dB when the singer is away from the mic. Most problems occur not when the singer is singing, but when she moves her head, which is serving as a great blockade against all the high-end leakage. Set the expander, which acts very much like a gate but with a little different feel, to have no effect when the singer is singing but to kick in and drop the level as much as is needed when the singer leaves the mic.

I will warn you that this technique is not for everyone. It is extremely tough to set the threshold at a level that works effectively to gate out high-end bleed but which also lets the spoken or low-level vocal passages through. I suggest that you disengage the expander/gate when the singer is speaking to the audience between songs, and re-engage it again when the next song starts. It may take some work, but it can pay off by allowing you to boost a little more high end than you would normally be able to get away with. Just remember that if the gate is set too tight certain vocal phrasing may be unnaturally cut off, so be ready to start with a very loose gate/expander and tighten it up a little at a time.

I came across this process through the suggestion of a fellow sound engineer on a multi-act tour. I was whining one day about the fact that the singer had very low throat output and every time I tried to add some zip to his vocal EQ, I picked up the highs from everything on stage. I tried the above mentioned expander method for a while and it worked with inconsistent regularity. I wrote down this trick because I felt it was worth mentioning, just in case someone tries this and finds it to be the pot of gold at the end of the rainbow, but I don't expect it to work for everyone, every time. As I said, it worked well in this one situation, but not every time I have tried it. Give it a go, and see what comes of it.

"STAND BACK, SHE'S GONNA BLOW!"

Inspired by every great crew I've worked with

OK. When all hell is breaking loose, what are you going to do? Your backup plan is the subject of this memo.

What are the main things in the show that just can't go away for very long without being sorely missed? I would have to take a not-so-daring guess and say the lead vocal. So your plan is to have a backup wireless mic and also a hard wire coiled up neatly ready to send out if the backup RF doesn't work. Right? Of course you do.

In all my days I've never had to go to the wired mic, but it's great to have it there anyway. Alrighty then, how about the kick drum mic? When a kick goes away it's pretty bad, so as I've suggested before, have a second mic in the drum to use as a backup (as well as an option for more artistic mixing). But we're not talking about art now by golly, we're all about panic and mayhem and solutions and hero medals. Ok, how about effects? If you have a main effect that you just can't do without, have a copy of that effect on another unit ready to go in case of a crash and burn. It may be a snare verb or the 'gotta have it' lead vocal reverb or delay. Just have it backed up and available.

Some things may not be so easily backed up. You can't change out a keyboard or guitar amp without there being some kind of delay, but just as every backline technician has a spare keyboard or guitar for his guy, you should have spares for the things that matter most. This goes for as many mics, EQs, effects, and processing as you can get the budget to cover. It doesn't always go over really well, but if you use an effect only once in the night for some special effect it is worth checking it, so that it is in the rack for a backup for something more important. The next topic is to have a pre-discussed game plan with the stage technicians to find the fastest, most effective way to swap out a problem on stage. If everyone is on the same page, the panic level stays at a minimum and clearer heads prevail.

The first issue should be communication. Everyone should be able to talk to each other via intercom or walkie-talkie. At this stage of the game the change should be made with everyone on board, front-of-house and monitor engineers, and stage techs knowing what is happening and ready to mute and un-mute as needed. A smooth change without any glitches makes everyone look good, which brings us to our next point. Have the backup vocal mics tested and dialed in on a daily basis. It is easy to forget these things in the daily soundcheck. If you hand the lead vocalist a new mic and it sounds terrible to him, you are going to shake his confidence in the mic, and you, at the same time. Even if you get the original back and working, it can sometimes be enough to throw the rest of the night's rhythm off in a span of five minutes. So like a Boy Scout, be prepared. Have the tools, equipment, and game plan in place to make a speedy swap and you and the whole audio team will look like champs, as well as top notch Emergency Rescue Technicians. "Everyone can return to your seats now, the situation is under control."

CHAPTER 18

Intelligent Mixing

It seems we're back to this thinking thing again. Let me remind you that if you wanted to shut your brain off while on the job, you could be employed in the kind of trade where the toughest question you must ask each day is: Regular or supersize?

So let's put our thinking caps back on. This time it pertains to mixing the show. There will be many decisions and judgment calls that will need to be made during the course of the show, none involving burgers and fries, and you'll have to deal with the data at the same time you're pushing faders. Despite all your preparations during the day, show conditions often don't reflect what you had prepared for. If you think the sound of the room has drastically changed from soundcheck or something is just not right, your intuition is probably correct. Between you and your sound-system check, some investigation may be in order. Meteorological conditions and many screaming fans can cause you to rethink things quite a bit. Take a moment or two and think it through.

But before you do, read on and think through these notes first. They will help you to expect the unexpected and handle it better when it comes your way.

"WITH SPECIAL GUESTS, THE GUINEA PIGS"

4/30/95 Van Halen

Okay let's be honest. You may think your dreams have come true the day you receive the awesome news that your band is going to get an opening act slot on the big rock tour that's hitting the road. This is indeed good news by most accounts, but a little dose of reality strikes new acts when they find that things are not always as posh out there being the opener as they might have been being the big fish in the little pond called the club scene. Everything from dressing room food to a lack of towels can leave you feeling a little less than important.

This often trickles all the way down to your soundcheck time, or complete lack thereof. There's the ruthless front-of-house mixer for the headline act who leaves you, as the opening act mixer, with a whopping total of three noise gates and two compressors. Then he says, "Oh, you need a reverb unit? No you don't, I've done this room before and it's really live." You get the picture. His last stake to the heart is to use your 50-minute set as the final tune-up of the EQ and level balance of the PA so that his precious headliner comes out sounding right as rain.

You could have gone to school for 15 years to become a brain surgeon, but you thought twisting knobs would be a far more glamorous lifestyle. Well, here you are, wallowing in the glitz and glory of our sound engineering profession. Just be sure to be cataloging all the slimy little tricks the headline engineer is testing on you, and promise to pay back another opening act mixer when you get to be the head honcho. And to all you headline artist mixers out there, well done. Walk the room and get things balanced while they're playing their meaningless set. This will also help you gauge how the room has changed now that the audience is in the seats (well, at least 50 of the 15,000 seats).

Everyone knows that while the opener is on everyone is still at the concession stands buying headliner t-shirts, or out in the parking lot playing the headliner's CD on their car stereos. I mean, no one really cared about, or even heard of the Guinea Pigs until the headline band was generous enough to give them a spot on the colossal rock tour you are mixing, anyway. Just be sure to have a great sounding show after using the opening act mixer as your test pilot, because if you don't, he'll be sure to tell all his band mates how his mix blew yours away, and how you must have gotten the job because the bass player is your brother.

7/22/97 Ted Nugent

We are asked to go into some pretty crazy rooms around this world and make the PA system sound good for everyone in the house. This isn't always easy, and with budgets the way they are today we are not always given the tools do make it great for everyone. One way that we can keep from sabotaging some of the tougher rooms is to keep a close watch on what we're panning hard left and right. Some rooms are set up with a short throw from the stage and very wide side seating for the audience. Unfortunately, with this situation, many of the audience members are only hearing one side of the sound system. This can really give them an odd mix if you have certain things panned really wide.

Instruments like keyboards, which mostly have the same information going left and right but are utilizing both sides to spread things out in the stereo spectrum, will usually not give you too much trouble. Some things like percussion tracks often have some things panned very wide, and only to one side, so if you pan those returns hard left and right the whole right side of the audience may not hear a hi-hat that is panned way left. This is the same for toms. We all love to mix in the center of the room and hear a drum roll move from our right to our left, but if you pan this really wide and you're sitting way off to one side it sounds really weird.

Another venue type that is notorious for this kind of thing is the racetrack grandstand setup. A lot of times the grandstand is very close to the stage but the seats are very wide. In one of these situations I was forced to mix right in front of one of the stacks of speakers and the house right stack was eighty feet over to my right and completely inaudible from where I was. In this kind of situation I ended up panning everything straight up in the middle and it made me wonder how many times that person sitting off to the sides was hearing odd stereo abnormalities. This situation caused me mix a lot less stereo-heavy from then on. I pan things that are pretty much the same left and right, but uneven stereo mixes get a much closer to middle channel assignment these days. It's great to sit in your big comfy chair and listen to the big stereo, but keep in mind that only a very small percentage of the crowd is hearing things the same way.

"TAKE ME DOWN SLOW AND EASY"

7/2/96 Gin Blossoms

One of the joys of summer touring is the festival season. Along with sunshine and plenty of sweaty, adoring fans comes the life-changing experience of mixing on everybody else's sound system but your own. One common protective practice used by the system's techs on these PAs is an early and sometimes maddening amount of compression on the entire system. I don't blame these techs for doing this, as I've witnessed plenty of Samurai sound engineers who like nothing better than to turn these rigs into one large confetti cannon.

If you've had trouble staying out of the main compression placed across these sound systems (equipped with a previously described system tech who is a little more cautious than he needs to be), you might want to consider inserting a compressor of your own across your kick and/or snare drum to knock down some of the peaks that might be inadvertently killing your overall level. If you're already doing this you are correctly thinking that keeping the overall signal from your console consistent and tight will give you more headroom. However, if you find that you sometimes have great success and other times you do not, I would like to suggest that you try a slower attack time on that kick and snare compressor. By slowing the time that the compressor reacts to a very loud hit you will still get the lowering of level that you are looking for, but it won't kill that transient crack you still would like to hold on to. You'll get a more even result and hopefully keep some of the attack on those important instruments. Staying out of the main system compression as much as possible is vital. If you keep the overall signal from your console "un-transient," or level controlled, you will be able to just tickle the system compression and get the most bang for the system's buck.

8/3/97 Ted Nugent

The height of the riser upon which you're mixing the show can vastly affect the amount of high end you're hearing at the mix position. During the summer touring season problems of varying riser heights seem to be a little more prevalent. With all the open field shows and state fair venues, you never know where your mix position may be.

What happens so often in these situations is that a laser beam of high end melts the person mixing the show if the riser is more than three feet in the air. When they are over five or six feet, you can really get a misrepresentation of what the majority of the crowd is hearing. During one show the problem was so bad that I had the representative from the sound company turn down high-end drivers at the amplifiers for the speakers that were pointing at the mix position. I walked around the open-air field while the opening act was on and noticed that the PA sounded very dull just about everywhere except the very front, where the speakers were just a few feet away. I went up to have a listen at the front-of-house mix position and as I climbed the stairs at the back of the five-foot riser I noticed the high end increase as I gained altitude. By the time I got up to the mixing board, the highs were on set to "stun." The front-of-house mixer either didn't mind it or was fighting it and not winning.

The problem seemed to be that the five-foot increase in height over the average listening level of the crowd put the mixers right in the path of the high-end horn pattern at a level far hotter than on the ground. By turning the high-end horns down and eventually off, the problem only got slightly better at front of house and only worsened the already-dull audience listening area. One lesson learned was that I tried to fix the problem too late in the day. If I had spotted the extra high end at the mix position earlier in the day, I may or may not have been able to make changes to help the situation, but I would at least have had the time to try several options.

Be sure to have a listen everywhere when you tune the PA and take into account how things might be different at the mix position. You may or may not be able to make PA changes to even things out, but the point is to get your reference at front of house and adjust EQ accordingly to make the majority of the room or field sound as evenly balanced as possible. When you see the tall mix riser, be careful!

"WHAT ARE YOU REFERRING TO?"

8/3/97 Ted Nugent

It's all about reference. It doesn't seem too long ago that all we asked of our PAs was to get good and loud so that everyone on the mix riser would be ooohing and aaahing at the thunderous sub-bass and kickin' mix. The problem was that very often the rest of the room didn't sound much like the mix position.

There were various reasons for this, one being the lack of attention to hanging or stacking the PA in a manner that made the whole room sound somewhat like the mix position. It appears that lately that much more mind is paid to the fine art of balancing a room with proper zoning of your PA as well as careful and thorough EQ'ing and volume balancing. Once the sound engineer and system tech feel the room is as consistent as it can be, the mixer can concentrate on mixing. An unfortunate situation does occasionally come up where the mix position has considerably more high-end content than the rest of the listening audience, due to a high mix riser or a host of other reasons.

This happened to me on a recent occasion and I did something I never thought I'd ever do mixing a show: I put in earplugs. It took some time to find the right percentage of dampening (by way of adjusting how loose or how tight the plugs sat in the ear canal), but after deciding that placing the foam plugs on end just inside my ear opening made the best change to my listening reference, I left them there all night and had much more success. The test was then to step off the high riser I was mixing on; upon hitting the ground, I entered the general listening area of the crowd and pulled the plugs out to check how I was doing. Before putting the plugs in, the field area (it was an open-air field venue) was very dull because I had pulled out quite a lot of high end at the EQs to make things right where I was mixing from.

Unfortunately, I was the only one hearing all that high end and therefore I was EQ'ing for one person instead of the eight thousand or so that were there. By putting the foam plugs in loosely, I was able to flatten the high end considerably at the mix position and make things better overall without killing myself at the console. The problem was that my reference was way off. I was mixing in a bright zone and the crowd was not in that zone. The solution in those situations is to make the audience area right and try to compensate your listening reference to make the right EQ choices.

"IF YOU CAN'T BEAT IT, CHEAT IT"

4/24/95 Van Halen

There are days when we are blessed with a decent room to mix in, and then there are those other days. The kind of day when you walk into a room and try to get a feel for the sound, and then someone closes a case lid with a loud crash and any chance at a warm, fuzzy feeling goes right out the door. The sound reverberates around the room for about ten seconds, and you get a pretty clear idea right then what kind of day you're in for. The main thing to think about at this point is that they can't all sound great, and every sound engineer that has come through this room has had the same challenge, and has probably had mixed results.

The trick is to see what the room is going to give you, and then work *with* it, not against it. When you are in a room that is very reverberant, there is a tendency for things to sound muddy, with lots of midrange and low end rolling around, and this makes it tough to distinguish the various instruments from each other. In an attempt to overcome this, the immediate reaction is often to turn things up, to give things some clarity over the roar of the hall. While this may sometimes work, another approach is to turn the overall volume down and accentuate the high-mid and high-end frequencies on the various instruments and vocals. This gives them some crispness and cut to add to the already-thick midrange and low-end hang time.

This method will help to keep the room from being over-excited in the area where its natural reverb time is the longest; most often, this is the mid and low end. On the other end of the spectrum, there are rooms that are very dry and lifeless. In this group are various open-air outdoor venues. In these rooms, the mix appears to have no warmth and oomph because there are either dead surfaces (heavily carpets or drapes) or no reflective surfaces (in the case of open-air gigs). In these cases, I suggest doing a thorough job of EQ'ing the high-mid and high-end section of the PA to cut out the bitey frequencies, and then turning up the overall level a bit with a touch of low-end boost. This will help to over-accentuate the bottom-end rumble that we get used to hearing with big PAs, and help to keep things nice and smooth. Try to overcome the room; don't let it overcome you.

"ONE-SIDED"

10/14/97 Engelbert Humperdinck

In a perfect world, sound engineers would always mix in the middle of the listening area and there would never be any low end lobbing to bother us when we mix. Since this isn't a perfect world, it is very important to be sure that what you're hearing way off to one side is also happening on the other side of the room. There have been situations where entire banks of speakers have gone down during a show and I didn't even know it until someone in the crowd (or one of my techs) came up to tell me. This is all because the club owner or promoter could sell more seats by making me mix next to the bar. What I like to do in these situations is to be very sure when I turn on the PA in the morning that everything is working, and then do as much EQ'ing from the center of the room as possible.

After that is done, you simply have to trust that most people are hearing something similar to what you are hearing. Right before the show starts it's always a good idea to walk around the various zones of PA and be sure everything is on and working. For the show it is imperative that you have a trusted assistant around who can walk the room and confirm that everything is functioning, and offer small EQ suggestions (if you trust him that much). It's a bit of a scary situation to know that you can only hear one side of the PA, and if something happens on the other side you may not even know it. Be sure you have concerned, qualified helpers around who can help keep your mind at ease by doing periodic checks of the other half of the room. You can then get down to the business of mixing the show.

"HEY, DID YOU HEAR SOMETHING?"

9/27/95 Van Halen

Most of the time a fair bit of consideration is given to putting the mixing board in a position where you have a relatively decent chance of hearing well. There are also those situations when people stand up on seats in front of you and it gets a little tougher, but usually you have at least a reasonable line of sight and hearing avenue to the speakers. The rare occasion arises when all the obstacles are against you and you have little or no reference at the mix position to the way that it sounds in the majority of the venue.

A situation occurred a while back when we were doing an outdoor show in Denver at an open-air venue in late September. It started snowing at about noon that day and continued on all through the show. We had a total of approximately 9 inches of snow and therefore had to pull the retractable roof over the mix position to keep the equipment dry. The problem worsened when the 2-foot opening in front of me, through which I had to see and hear the band, was completely blocked by people standing on their seats. I was in a totally sound-isolated situation where my reference at the board was completely different than what was really going on. When I crawled out of the sound bunker to have a listen it was about 10dB louder and much brighter than it was at the mixing board.

The only solution was to turn back around, settle in, and just mix the way I had been mixing all through the tour. Of course, this only works if you've been mixing the band for a while and you have a good idea of the mix moves that you do each night. If it's a first time mix with a new band things are going to be much scarier.

The main concern is getting the frequency response of the PA as close as you can to normal when you stick your head above the roof and crowd. Take a walk out and have a listen. Go back and make the necessary EQ changes and then take another walk back to the real world. After a few trips you can be reasonably sure that the PA is tuned in a way that you would normally tune it. After that your job is just to mix the show from memory, miming the fader moves and cues. It really helps at this point if you have paid attention in the past to where your mixing board's meters have been running during the show. If the master fader and the group and channel faders are at their usual spot, you should be fine.

The toughest thing is avoiding a mix that is too bright. When you are severely blocked from the speakers, things are usually quite dull and the tendency is to brighten it up. When this urge strikes, take another walk up top and have a listen. You will probably have a few spots where things from the crowd's perspective are a little off. There may be bright piercing frequencies that you're just not hearing. But for the most part, if you tuned the PA to be balanced in the afternoon, and you make global changes during the show, you can do a pretty decent job. Just remember to mix for what's going on out there, and not where you are.

CHAPTER 19

Weather

Everybody sing now: "Mixing in the rain, just mixing in the rain…"

God bless Mother Nature. We have to deal with her every day of our lives. Hot in the summer, cold in the winter. Knowing a trick or two and just being prepared can turn your dark skies to blue, so don't feel all stormy inside. Close the blinds, warm up the fire, pull a warm blankie over you and dive into the next section. Pretty soon the sun will be shining again. Oh, and save a hot chocolate for me, would you?

"SUMMERTIME BLUES"

8/3/95 Van Halen

Ahhh, the sun, the heat, the barbecues, the parking lot parties…and the rain.

The summer touring season often has us working and mixing in less-than-desirable surroundings. A lot of outdoor venues, especially in the United States, have large coverings over the stage and mix/audience area, but often times we'll be out in a field somewhere or at a race track. When rain is pouring down and the wind is blowing, things can change quite drastically. Strong winds blowing give the perception that the high end is swirling around, and the volume of the mix will jump from quiet to loud very quickly. Humidity changes also can affect the sound by altering the level of high end making it to the seats and drastically changing the distance the sound travel outdoors. A cool, crisp night will often create high-end "zingers" in the PA and monitors, as those upper frequencies become more predominant. A nice sunny soundcheck can be totally useless come show time if everything—wind, rain, temperature, and humidity—has changed.

Remember to always trust your ears. It's very easy to start second guessing what you are now hearing and say to yourself: "This was fine earlier," or "It didn't sound like this before." Just mix it the way you hear it. Be flexible and know that nothing is the same as it was at soundcheck. Remember that in the wind the high end will blow around considerably. Try to pick the calmest moments as your reference and then don't worry if things fluctuate between bright and muddy. You can only be responsible for the things you can control. Most likely, if it's raining on stage, or at least on the downstage edge, the band members and their techs are scrambling around trying to keep things dry just as much as you are.

We always try to grab a couple rolls of plastic sheeting (visquene) if we see the dark clouds rolling our way. If it's obvious we're going to get wet, my systems tech will grab a couple of stage hands and start battening down the hatches by preparing the mix area with a plastic roof and walls while the show is going on. If the rain starts to fall we'll cover up as much gear as we can while still allowing me to mix. Unless they call the show for weather—and you'd be surprised how often they don't—the show must go on. Hang in there and try against all odds to concentrate on what's going on up on stage. Oh ya, and always have plenty of plastic sheeting around.

"WRAP THAT, I'LL HAVE IT TO GO"

7/23/95 Van Halen

All of us who have toured in the winter and loaded trucks in sub-zero weather dream of the days when the sun is shining and the gigs are fun again. Yes, summer touring is my favorite time of year, but there are those pesky bad weather days that really make things ugly. There are things we can do to be prepared for the afternoon thunderstorms that always seem to happen right around soundcheck time. As I said above, always have plenty of plastic sheeting around to cover up mixing boards and all the other things that don't like rain.

One other thing to have on hand is a roll of Saran Wrap or other such plastic sandwich wrap. Why? Well, it does tend to keep your lunch from getting wet, but it is also good to keep water off microphones and monitor wedges. The amazing thing about it is that almost all of the sound, including the high end, manages to get through the sandwich wrapping while water tends to stay out. It's another modern wonder of science. Amen, I say.

In the old days, as soon as the rain showers started to fall, we would flip the wedges over on the downstage edge. If a band happened to be playing while the rain shower ensued, you had the choice of letting the band hear what they were playing and potentially destroying your speakers, or flipping them over for protection. Well, a temporary quick fix is here. By wrapping your speakers and microphones in Saran Wrap you can continue on with little noticeable difference in sound quality. Take that, Mother Nature.

"TWO WAYS TO LOOK GOOD AT FRONT OF HOUSE"

6/28/97 Ted Nugent

None of us like to see those big black rain clouds roll in when we're doing an outdoor show. As the ominous moisture demons move in, a small army of stagehands and techs start cutting plastic sheeting to prepare for the onslaught. The threat is often magnified at front of house due to the fact that a solid roof providing protection from the elements is not always a priority. One reason for this is the simple fact that a big roof over front of house often blocks sight lines when there are grandstands behind the riser, and promoters are trying to fill every seat. The only way to deal with this situation is to simply be as prepared as possible.

Have some essential weapons available to do battle with the elements. Let me say again that a roll of plastic sheeting is a necessity. Setting up a game plan for quickly bungee strapping a plastic tarp or makeshift roof and walls should be considered (or constructed and then rolled back) early, and having duct tape, bungee straps and a cutting knife around can never hurt. But what happens if the rain comes down and all your efforts seem to be failing as drops of water start to invade your little hut? It's good to have a few dry towels ready for dabbing water off the console, and very good to have a blow dryer available at front of house in case some water does get into the console and starts to mess with the electronics. You can often put a halt to any electronic glitches that may start as the water gets in by running the hot air over the areas of the board that get wet. Sometimes you may have to shut things down and pull out some channels to get the hot air right on the problem areas. Even if you have to stop the show for a short time, it's better to get the board working glitch free than to cancel the whole event.

Another thought is to have a game plan ready for potentially using the opening act's board to mix your headline act on. If you chart your gain structure and how it might translate to the other console, you can possibly swap over the input snake (if they are compatible) and finish up on the opener board. This is a last ditch effort to save the show, but it has happened to me. Once, at a very large show in Spain, an off-duty rocket scientist in the crowd wanted to see how a beer in a plastic cup would look hurtling through the air and landing on a $50,000 mixing board. In this situation we went right to work, swapping snake lines over to the opening act console and salvaged the show. As we went to work on the second console, the hair dryer went to work on the main board and helped to dry up some of the beer before it turned all the circuitry into a big sticky mess. This made us all look pretty good with our quick thinking and creative problem solving.

Oh, and the other way to look good, you ask? Use the hair dryer to give your hair a quick touchup after the summer thunderstorm.

"THTOP THPITTING ON THE MICTH"

11/6/92 Faith No More

Some microphones are very susceptible to moisture. It goes without saying that the more you spend on a microphone the better the sound you will receive in return, with a few exceptions. The flip side to the high-dollar unit is that you often get a microphone that is not as good at taking temperature and moisture fluctuations and will often give up the ghost or just sound lousy. For this reason there are certain standards of microphones in the live touring industry that have been road tested and seem to hold up to weather as well as a bump and bruise or two. The new breed of mics being manufactured these days is changing the course of things though. They are much tougher and still sound great. This doesn't mean that we shouldn't have a few extras around for those circumstances that put a mic through the ringer.

One thing that often happens through the course of a 90-minute or two-hour show is the spit build-up effect. A singer that happens to be a heavy spitter (in addition to a vocalist) can get that sponge pop filter inside the ball of the mic pretty soggy after a while. The sound of the mic will soon deteriorate to a less-than-acceptable standard and my advice is to change out the mic before you reach that point. After touring with that singer for a couple of weeks you should be able to determine the best spots in the show to change out the mic. The front-of-house and monitor guy can decide this together, and then have the vocal channel muted for the change. This practice should also be used when you are playing outdoors and rain begins to fall. If you think the mic is gathering a little water, run a fresh one out there once or twice and do yourself a favor. This is not always an option with certain singers and RF mics. They may use the same mic for 40 straight shows and, as the saying goes, "if you want this mic you'll have to pry it out of my cold dead hand." In those cases, you are left with no alternatives for maintenance during the show.

If you are able to make a switch, I would warn and advise against blow drying the mics to dry them off because of the diaphragms, but if you can unscrew the top ball that holds the pop filter you can give that a quick blast with the blow dryer and then try to let the rest of the mic get a little warm dry air overnight. One thing to always be sure of is that the mic you are going to run out on stage sounds good and similar to the one you are using, so things don't change drastically for the engineers and the vocalist. Remember that a dry mic is a happy mic.

CHAPTER 20

Politics

Interestingly enough, I write this intro the night after George W. Bush was finally given the title of president-elect of the United States of America. That should sufficiently set the stage for this section, which deals with the importance of politics. Not the politics of uncounted votes in the Sunshine State, but politics as it pertains to mixing a touring musical act. And believe me, there are plenty of political maneuvers going on each and every day of our lives out on the road as well.

From building your PA system and staying within a pre-conceived budget to dealing with differences in mixing philosophies among the band, manager, and yourself, there is plenty to lobby, debate, and vote about. You'll be called upon once or twice to present a brief outlining your reasons for proceeding in a particular direction and you'll no doubt discover the benefits of smiling brightly (and maybe even kissing a baby or two) to smooth things over with a promoter rep in hopes of making your day a little better.

There's political posturing and even the potential for legislation in our world, so be prepared to dodge an issue, answer a question with another question, and maybe even bend the truth now and then. It's the American way.

"THE DB POLICE"

6/26/93 Van Halen

Everyone has a different idea of what is loud enough and what is uncomfortably too loud. Usually, we as engineers are left pretty much alone to determine the SPL (sound pressure level) of the show we are mixing, but another determining factor is often the management of the band.

There have been situations where the artist's manager—who has found a cozy place to stand during the show: right over my shoulder—has told me that the show is just not loud enough. I tend to mix rock and roll shows at a level that I find comfortable yet powerful. This is not a Utopian dream. It can be done. Sometimes you will be faced with the situation of deciding if you want to stand up to management and keep it at a level that you think is safe and punchy, or if you want to risk a little hearing loss to give them what they're after.

The flip side to this situation is the "too loud" problem. This is a much more common scenario that goes on in just about every club in the world and many of the outdoor venues during the summer months. A lot of outdoor venues were built (or were originally located) and then became surrounded by residential areas, and the complaints come flooding in every show night. Some of the venues have gone to computerized SPL readouts and charting systems with a green, yellow, and red indicator light for the front-of-house sound engineer to gauge his level above and below the accepted mark. The charting of the ups and downs in sound level throughout the night is proof for the venue of what really went on the night of the show if the city commissions come calling for noise ordinance penalties.

Sometimes these dB limits are unbelievably strict and it seems silly to even put on a rock show when the sound of the acoustic drum kit from the stage, unamplified, is lighting up the warning lights (not to mention the audience applause). These situations do occur though, and we all must try to deal with them as they come along.

The way to best deal with this is through knowledge, patience, and an understanding of the chain of command. The club sound engineer knows all too well the restrictions he is put under to keep the volume down so that the bar staff can serve drinks with some level of communication. In this situation, I have always tried to have the head person from the band, whether it is a road manager or musician, get with the head person from the bar's management and discuss the procedure for volume limits and how an infringement will be handled. This goes for every level of artist, management, and sound engineer interaction.

I always try to have a discussion very early on in the day to verify who has the authority to enforce noise violations and who will be the one to come and tell me during the show. If a person I have never met before comes up during the show and tells me to turn it down, I will look that person in the face and mention that I have an understanding with so and so, and he has told me that he will be the only one to have communication with me. With big tours I have a policy of not even dealing with house management at any time during the show. If the management has a problem with volume, they are to go to my tour/production manager, who then tells my system tech, who then passes the word on to me. The buck usually stops long before me.

If everyone is aware of what those limits are going to be for that day, what will happen if a violation occurs, and who will be notified and in what manner, the level of communication is already at a state where cool heads can prevail. Now, you're sitting there thinking that in a bar situation, bringing up volume inquiries with the management before the band even begins playing will just send up red flags to the management that you intend to blow the doors off the place. I don't believe this to always be the truth. Try to be friendly and assure the management that you are not a maniac and that you are willing to go along with his volume restrictions, but you like to know in advance the procedure that will take place if he thinks it's getting too loud. Keep communications open and let the musicians know what is going on so that they can decide if playing under unreasonably low volume conditions is something they want to do in that venue.

Nobody likes to have his or her head blown off at a show, and unfortunately it has happened too many times and hurt the rest of us who don't let that happen very often. The secret to a good starting point is to balance the PA so that you are hearing the same sort of level that everyone else in the venue is hearing and then controlling those frequencies that tend to bite. We're all in this together, and if management and sound engineers don't keep a lid on volume levels, government agencies are going to start controlling what we do and this could make it tough for us to mix a powerful rock show ever again.

4/19/98 Van Halen

Varying acoustical properties within different venues can be very deceiving when it comes to the volume of the show you're mixing. Sometimes a very live room will give you the impression that the SPL level of the show is much higher than it really is, because there is so much reflected sound making the direct sound harder to distinguish. The overall confusion to the ears makes things seem louder. Conversely, when you are mixing in a very acoustically dead room you may find yourself going for the gas pedal a little more, even though your SPL meter is showing that you are at your regular show level. For this reason (and a couple others), I like to keep an SPL meter handy to give me a reference. I will usually put it in the "A" weighting mode, with a medium to slow response time, which gives me a general, average reading. Most volume enforcement organizations will read things "A" weighted (SPL measured with a slight consideration for low end giving you a lower reading than B or C weighting), so I like to as well. Most discussions concerning volume will naturally take the "A" weighted level as a reference.

Some Real Time Analyzers have a digital meter to let you know what your SPL is, and by glancing occasionally over at it during the show I can be fairly certain that I'm where I want to be. It's a good idea to make sure your metering device has been calibrated to the microphone that is measuring SPL and then double check with a couple other meters. I had a situation recently while mixing a loud arena rock band where the tour manager came over during one of the final shows of a year-long tour and asked if things were louder than normal. My systems tech directed his gaze to the LED readout and said "105! That's where we've been all year." The tour manager said "Oh, okay" and walked away. That was all he needed to know.

It is reassuring to everyone involved that there is a way to prove that nothing is different from the norm, and that the SPL level that makes the band, venue and majority of the audience happy is being monitored and paid attention to. It's a political and litigious world out there, and aside from mixing shows and providing great concert sound, we have to pay attention to keeping things safe for the listeners, which I try to do by mixing at a consistent level that is safe for two hours of exposure. By trying to make the volume in every seat the same as it is at the mix position, and then mixing at a safe level every night, I feel that I am keeping things in check. Without the meter I know I would occasionally second-guess the SPL level. With it, the proof is in the pudding.

"PLAY SMART, PLAY THE GAME"

5/23/94 Extreme

Most of us will be put in the position of mixing the opening act on a multi-act tour at some point in our careers. This can be a fun time, and with only 50 minutes each night to get things dialed in, it can be a bit of an adrenaline rush. Pulling things together right from the start of the show with little or no soundcheck is a real talent. You have so little time to get things dialed in to make the majority of the band's set sounds great.

An important factor in having a great sounding show is using the opening act mixing board (which is often provided so the headliner's console is not touched) to its fullest capacity. This means setting gain levels that work well within the parameters of crossover and drive settings that the headliner has defined. If you try to get your opening act to be considerably louder than the headliner by cranking up the output of your mixing board, chances are the system tech is going to slap a master compressor on your board's outputs, and pretty soon you'll be burying the needles with little or no payoff.

One way to get off to a good start is to set your console output at 0 dB on the master meters (with pink noise or a 1K tone) and have the headliner's console receive this signal at 0 dB on his end. This should mean that the level at which he is running his console to ensure good gain and headroom is pretty close to what you should have on your console. You should then try to set things up like you normally would so that your gain structure flows from section to section evenly, without any clipping. If you feel your show just has no punch at 0 dB on your masters, the best thing to do is to approach the system tech on a professional level and ask if you could receive a little more level on his end. Explain to him that you don't want to turn your console up any more and run the risk of slamming into clip. If you ask nicely, they should be accommodating, as long as you don't take this as license to turn things up a bunch and cause friction.

Playing the game while you are in the position of the underling on a big tour is very important. In my opinion, you will reap far more rewards doing it their way than trying to tell the headliner mixer and his system tech that you only play one way and they will just have to deal with it. If you play nice, you will most likely find your colleagues more willing to give you some leeway. If you don't feel like playing nice, you may find yourself being asked to leave the playground.

"THE POLITICALLY CORRECT MIX"

8/6/95 Van Halen

We in the audio business, like all other representatives of an esteemed profession, have values and ethics to provide the best service possible to the customer.

Now let's get back to the real world. We really do constantly try to mix a performance to please the crowd, and the artists do not always know what audio hoops we're jumping through to make their music the best it can be that particular night. Sometimes, though, we are forced to mix to please the artist. I will never claim that a sound engineer has a better idea of what the artist is trying to say with her music than the artist, or how that artist would like her music to be projected, but sometimes (not always) we know how to make something work in the world of audio better than the musician or band. The question is, when an artist comes out front to have a listen to the whole mix (or just his instrument) and doesn't like what he is hearing, how should this be handled?

The best approach is patience, humbleness, and the ability to take constructive or even non-constructive criticism and make the situation better. There have been times where I have witnessed an artist giving a sound engineer valid suggestion or criticism, and shortly after the artist's departure, that engineer has whispered under his breath about how musicians just don't understand sound, or just don't know what we're up against. (There have been other comments, too, but this is a G-rated book.) This is very often the case, but I have personally received very helpful suggestions from musicians that have led me to see things a different way, or to try a different approach that has ended up helping. The bottom line is to let the artist know that the success of the mix is the most important thing to you, and whatever means are used to achieve this end, are means you are willing to consider.

There are times when an artist will say something like, "If we brought in another 72 speaker cabinets for this 500 seat club, it would kick, man." Well, I can almost guarantee that that is the truth. The problem is that the club may not be able to hold another 72 speaker boxes and more may not necessarily be the answer. From a practical standpoint, is the band willing to spend the money to rent another 72 speakers to get a little more kick drum, or is there a compromise or alternate approach that might help? I suggest (without looking like you're always giving a negative response to the artist's needs) that you explain the options available for the various situations that might come up. Talking things through does not always work with every musician, but it's a good place to start.

When all the issues and suggestions have been sorted through during the soundcheck, I truly believe that come showtime, you alone have to mix the show and deal with acoustic challenges the way you see fit. The band has to trust you, and trying to achieve what the band is paying you to reinforce must sit right with you. Think about what they would want themselves to sound like, and then try to achieve that the way you know is best.

"THE POLITICALLY CORRECT MIX, PART 2"

8/6/95 Van Halen

The other aspect of mixing to please the band is making the management happy. They most certainly will be backstage after the show while you're wrapping up cables, and they'll either be singing your praises or asking the band why they keep sending you a paycheck. Giving management the feeling that you are providing a great service to the band by mixing a great show night after night is very important. It also helps if you get along well with these people, so try to be respectful of the people who sign your check.

One thing that tends to happen in some rooms is that the mix, as perceived at the mixing console area, is not a real good representation of what is happening throughout the room, where the paying customers are seated. The usual compromise in this situation is this: You have to know how the changes you make at the mixing board will affect the area where most of the people are hearing the show, and then live with a mix at the console that may not be exactly the way you would like to hear it. Making the greater part of the room sound good should be your primary goal. Now comes the politically correct part. Most managers and people of influence, like possible future clients, stand at the mix area to watch and hear the show. This area is usually kept clear of unruly audience members and offers the best vantage point to observe.

When the situation involves a manager hearing your mix for the first time, or you're mixing a very important gig, I suggest you bend the rules of ethics and make the mix at the sound-board (or wherever they are observing from) the best it can be. The mix may suffer a little bit in other parts of the room, but for the time that they may be standing somewhat close to you, you should strive to make things really happening right where you are. The real and obvious answer is to always do your best to make every part of the room sound the same, and just as great as the mix position, but real life says that this does not always happen. Be a little bit flexible and please the important people too, they may be the ones signing your next check, not the people in nosebleed section 300.

"LADIES AND GENTLEMEN OF THE JURY..."

9/12/95 Van Halen

There are several reasons why I don't like making board tapes of the show. One reason is that while I'm mixing the show I tend to think about what's going to tape instead of what I'm doing in the room, and the mix for the room is all that really matters, if you think about it. Another reason is that a week after making a board tape, after I've long forgotten the sound of the room where the tape was made, I'll sit down to listen to the tape and question the EQ or mix moves I was doing and possibly rethink things in the future. The beauty of live sound mixing is that the mix is here and now and you must live in that domain. If you begin to think about something that is going to tape, you take something away from the way every second of every live song just needs to be mixed in the present.

That brings me to the third reason I don't like board tapes. The musicians in the band will listen to tapes and hear inconsistencies from one tape to another and wonder just what it is you're up to out there. It's perfectly legal under the employee/employer relationship to request each night's board tapes, but this must come with some level of understanding from the musicians who listen to them. They must trust you to begin with or you shouldn't be mixing their show. If they do trust you, then they need to give you the freedom to make whatever EQ changes and mix moves on the board that are needed to make the room sound the best. Things can turn out to be very thin sounding on a console board tape if the room was very boomy and you reached for low-end cut on channel EQ all night long. If you have the presence of mind to always make the changes to your system EQ and never touch your console EQ, then I tip my hat to you. While the system EQ should be the thing that changes every day to make your mix translate from room to room, in the heat of battle I don't always think of the correct way to do things, just the way that will make it happen right now.

Try not to let the band judge your abilities as a live sound mixer by your board tapes. Take the time to explain the process that goes on between system and console EQ, and what you often do to the console to make things work on the fly. Have them listen to their instrument through the PA or have a reputable friend stand by the console and give his opinions to the band (although this is dangerous in itself) but try to keep the dreaded board tape from being your judge and jury. Remember too, not to fall into the good tape-bad tape trap. If they say the tape sounded great and you reply, "that's just the way it sounds out front," you know this will come back to bite you. Be your own attorney, and explain things clearly so you can be acquitted of all charges.

Glossary

A-weighted—An audio level measurement standard which takes less low-end energy into account. Since low-end energy is often more pleasing to the ear at a music concert, measuring the show's level "A-weighted" gives a slightly lower "loudness" reading than B or C-weights and is therefore the preferred reading of most sound engineers for the level of the show.

Ambience/Ambient Noise—Natural surrounding noise. Sometimes used to describe the sound other than the intended sound that enters a mic or distracts the listener.

Array—A group or cluster of speakers. Used to describe the way a speaker system is set up to best cover the seating and listening area of the venue.

Attack—The initial impact of a signal. For example, the "crack" of a drum being hit. Also, the control function of a compressor or limiter that adjusts that unit's reaction to the signals initial impact.

Attenuation—The decrease of signal level. On a mixing console, the "attenuation" knob (also known as the "gain" knob) is often the first knob to be adjusted on a channel. It can set the incoming signal to a usable level before moving on the equalization and other adjustments.

Aux—Short for Auxiliary. This term is most often used to describe an output bus that gathers the individual send from each channel on the console. An example is an effects send. If you turn up "Aux 1" on each of the drum channels in an effort to send those drums to a reverb unit, the combined send will be grouped at the "Aux 1" output knob or fader and route from there to the input of the reverb device.

Balanced—A method of wiring that rejects hum and RF interference in cables. Also, often used in this text to describe even level between various zones of a sound system.

Bass—Low frequency information. Also, a musical instrument (bass guitar). Sound engineers are most often accused of undermixing this instrument, even though they are also often accused of getting their jobs by being the brother of the bass player.

BG—Abbreviation for background vocals.

Clip/clipping—The act of introducing a signal that is too strong for a console channel input, amplifier input, etc. The result is a distorted output signal. Usually indicated on your mixing board by a lot of flashing red lights.

Compression—The process of reducing the dynamic range of an input signal. Or, limiting the output level of an instrument or vocal's input. By using a compressor, you can keep a signal's level from going from too quiet to too loud.

Crossover—A device that divides a full frequency input signal into bands of audio suitable for specific speakers and high-end drivers. This device makes sure only highs go to the high end drivers, optimizing and protecting each component.

Cue—A button on a mixing console that gives the sound engineer an opportunity to listen to an individual signal by itself. Also known as Solo or PFL (pre-fade-listen). By pressing the cue button on a channel of the board, you are able to hear that input in headphones or speakers clearly and separately. Also a Cue can be a specific move to make during the show, such as pushing a fader up during a guitar solo, or un-muting some vocal mics.

Cut—Lowering the level of an input's signal or lowering certain frequencies by using an equalizer. Also, a phrase to describe a signal's ability to be heard above the surrounding noise, as in "cutting" through. Also, what will happen to your salary if you can't mix a drink, let alone a band.

dB—Abbreviation for decibel. The units of measurement for electronic and sound pressure quantities. Meters on your console will display signal in + or – dB values, and the volume of your mix will be measured in dB SPL (Sound Pressure Level).

Decay—The portion of the signal that follows the attack and slowly drops in level. With a tom-tom, the decay is the amount of time the drum takes to drop below the level we can hear it.

Delay—A device used to perform one of two functions. One is to align components such as mid speakers and high-end drivers within a speaker box, or an entire group of speakers with another group of speakers to line up arrival times. Secondly, a delay or DDL (digital delay line) can be used as an effect on a vocal or instrument to add depth and character. Oh ya, thirdly, this is what the artist can do to the start of the show to run up union labor costs and ensure you get even less sleep.

DI—An electronic box that converts the signal from a high impedance device like a guitar or keyboard to mic or line level, suitable to drive the input of a console. This is what you plug your bass guitar into to be heard in the PA.

Dry—A slang term used to describe a signal that has no effects (such as reverb and delay) on it.

Dynamic—Two separate definitions. One-A type of mic that moves a coil of wire through a magnetic field. This is the most common kind of mic we use in pop/rock music. Second-dynamic can be used to describe a signal that has the potential to go from very quiet to very loud. A mix that is has a lot of "punch" and yet quiets down wonderfully is said to be dynamic.

EQ—Short for equalizer or equalization. The process of altering or adjusting the tonal characteristics of an input or output signal. EQ can be used to compensate for speaker shortcomings or room abnormalities. It can also be used as an effect. EQ is often used as a Band-Aid and should be considered carefully before applying.

Expander—A signal processing device used to increase a signal's dynamic range. Its most common use is to reduce an input's level during quiet passages. For example, apply an expander to a vocal to reduce unwanted noise that enters the mic between phrases being sung.

Feedback—The archenemy of everyone in audio (except some guitar players). A phenomenon created when the sound leaving a loudspeaker is picked up by the microphone and then fed back into the loudspeaker again…and again back into the mic…etc, creating a loop which increases in volume every time and eventually squeals or squawks. Also known as a "Monitor mixer solo." I'm proud to have a few "solos" on a live record or two as a Monitor mixer.

Flat—A term to describe all frequencies at equal volume or amplitude. Also used to describe a sound system that is tuned to be pleasing to the ear and include all frequencies at apparently equal level. A "flat" curve such as this would have more energy in the low-end and gradually decrease as the frequency increases.

Fly—To "fly the PA" means to hang the speakers from motors and grids from the ceiling of the venue. This can be done singularly but more recently, speakers are flown in arrayed clusters on each side of the stage and in delay zones.

FOH—Abbreviation for "front of house." Used to describe the location out in the audience where the mixing console is located. Home Sweet Home.

Frequency—The number of complete cycles of a sound in a second. Measured in Hertz. We use this term often to recognize the pitch of a burst of feedback or tonality of a sound. E.g. 250 Hz is the frequency that is too loud in that vocal sound. Learning to associate the pitch of a note and associate it with a frequency is very important.

Gain—A term to describe how much a signal is amplified. Also, a knob on a console that performs the function of raising or lowering the gain of an input or output signal.

Gate—Also, Noise Gate, a signal-processing device used primarily to stop unwanted noise from entering a microphone. With drums, gates are used to keep mics "closed" until the drum in question is struck. Also used to control the decay time of the drum to tailor tonality.

Graphic EQ—An equalizer that uses sliders to perform the boost and cut functions at (usually) 1/3 octave increments. This EQ is often quicker and easier to use than a Parametric EQ, but can be less accurate and has limited flexibility.

Ground Stack—A group of speakers that is stacked on the stage or audience level floor. This is the way it was always done before motors were incorporated to fly the system from the roof. In some instances ground stacking works better, but flying the system most often achieves the best results because the speakers are further from the audience and a more even volume coverage occurs.

Group (subgroup)—A collection of two or more inputs on a console that can be controlled (level, EQ) by one fader or knob. An effective use of grouping is inserting compressors or eq into the whole group and consolidating equipment.

Headroom—The difference between the average operating level of the system and the level at which that system will "clip."

Hertz—The unit used to measure frequency. Abbreviated Hz. (and kHz meaning kilohertz or a thousand Hz.) One Hz represents one cycle per second.

High Pass Filter—Usually in the form of a knob on a mixing board's channel inputs. Its function is to attenuate low-end frequencies on the input signal. You will often be designated a frequency where this rolling-off begins to occur, but more expensive boards give the option of selecting the frequency at which the filtering of low-end begins. Useful on inputs such as cymbals and vocals.

House—The venue in which the performance is occurring. Also, "in the house" refers to audio that has to with the main speakers and not the monitor system. FOH (front of house) refers to the mixing area in the audience area.

In phase—When two signal combine to reinforce each other, they are said to be in phase. Correct phasing and polarity are extremely important to insure efficient output of speakers and electrical devices. Much can be said in a technical way about this, but if your mixing board has a "phase" or "polarity" switch and you are combining two like signals, always check for reinforcement rather than deterioration of the signal.

Insert—A patch point on a mixing console where a signal processing device such as a compressor or equalizer can be "inserted" into the signal path. Usually in the form of a single (or pair of) female connector but occasionally two XLR connectors are used.

Java—Otherwise known as coffee. Absolutely necessary to make it through a show, although you should carefully consider the pre-show consumption to length of show ratio.

Level—A term used to describe the strength or volume of a signal. There are three types of levels most common in audio:

- Mic level—Average level that comes from a microphone. Requires a pre-amp to make it usable at the mixing board.
- Line level—Standard audio levels. Usually in the +4dBu or –10dBV region.
- Instrument level—Average signal from musical instruments. Can be anywhere from low mic level to very hot line level.

Maybe not easy to understand now but very important when making equipment work together.

Line Check—A procedure that involves the FOH mixer, monitor mixer and one or more audio techs to check the integrity of each microphone and signal on stage. Usually occurs in the hours before the band arrives to insure all the lines are clean from buzzes and hums, and that they are making it to both mixing consoles at proper levels.

Low Pass Filter—The cousin of the High Pass Filter. This filter only passes lower frequencies and filters out high frequencies. See High Pass Filter for a more thorough description.

Main House Speakers (or Mains)—Refers to the largest clusters of speakers usually positioned just left and right of the stage.

Master—Usually in the form of a fader (or knob) on a mixing console. It is usually the final summing point of all the Groups and Subgroups on the mixer.

Matrix—An output section on some consoles that allow for the mixing of subgroups and master outputs to one output. For example, you can assign just the Stereo L/R outputs to Matrix 1 and 2 out. You can also add a little bit of the vocal subgroup to the Stereo L/R and assign that to Matrix 3 for a Front-fill mix that has vocals a little hot. Matrix mixes are great to use for delay outputs, under-balcony outputs in theatres and Record feeds.

Mic—Short for microphone, which is a transducer that converts acoustic energy into electrical energy which can be reinforced and processed by audio equipment.

Mixer—A piece of electronic equipment that combines multiple signals into one common output. Can be a very basic analog design to an extremely elaborate and expensive digital tool.

Monitor(s)—Speakers (or headphone/in-ear monitors) used on stage to help the performers hear themselves. Also refers to the area near the stage where the monitor mixes are done on the monitor console. A third description is a computer display.

Mute—A switch on a mixing board that turns something off, and then back on again. As a verb, to Mute is to turn off.

Near Field Monitors—Monitor speakers such as recording studios use that often sit on the top of the mixing board for headphone free listening by the audio mixer. They are great tools for line checking and isolating an instrument or vocal for analysis.

Noise Gate—See Gate

Out of Phase—Opposite of In Phase (see In Phase). When two signals combine with each other and cancel. The result is a serious loss of level, tonality or both.

PA—Public address system. A term used to describe our speakers and equipment as a whole. The whole pile of stuff together is the PA system.

Pad—An attenuator. On a console's input strip, a pad switch will reduce the overall level of the signal 20 or 30 dB. This is handy for microphones on guitars or very loud instruments that hit the input of the console really hard. By engaging the pad switch, you give yourself some play on the gain knob.

Pan Pot—A knob found on an input channel of a mixing console that is used to position the input in the stereo image. With a stereo PA system turning the Pan knob to the Left will position the instrument or vocal in the left speakers. With a Mono PA, Pan knobs are used in conjunction with Group Assign switches to choose which group to place the input in.

Parametric EQ—An equalizer that lets you adjust each "parameter" of a filter, those being center frequency, gain and bandwidth.

PFL—See Cue

Phantom Power—DC Voltage (usually +48V) that is sent down the mic cable from the mixing board to power a condenser mic or active DI box. The switch for phantom power is usually on the input strip of a console or can be found in separate phantom power supplies.

Phase—A term to describe how two signals, electrical or acoustic relate to one another. They will both combine and add in strength or volume (In Phase) or combine and deteriorate in strength or volume (Out of Phase).

Pink Noise—Electronically generated random noise that produces each octave of frequencies at equal level. The difference between white noise and pink noise is a 3dB per octave roll-off with pink noise that characterizes the way a human ear perceives loudness.

Pop Filter—A sponge filter that fits on the ball of vocal mics and condenser mics to reduce wind noise and percussive vocal sounds like "p" and "b."

Proximity Effect—The property of many mics whereby the low-end response increases as the source gets continually closer to the mic's element. The difference in low-end energy at 1 inch from the mic as compared to 6 inches can be remarkable. Also, proximity effect can be used to describe the cold clammy feeling you get when the Artist is staring over your shoulder during sound check as he/she listens to your mix.

Q—Used to describe the bandwidth of a filter. The higher the Q value, the narrower the bandwidth.

Return—A line input on a mixing console which is used to accept the output signal from a piece of signal processing gear that is inserted into a channel or subgroup. Also, a line level input on a console where various pieces of gear can input the mixer.

Reverberation—The sound that remains in a room after the source sound has stopped. Sometimes reverb adds warmth and character to a mix, but sometimes it is thick, which makes it difficult to hear the source mix clearly. Also, a digital effects unit used to create a spatial environment. Great on drums, horns and vocals.

RTA—Abbreviation for Real Time Analyzer. A device that gives a graphic display of the frequency response of the room or whatever signal is sent to the input. Extremely useful in helping to tune the PA to the room and for locating problem frequencies in monitors and house speakers.

Send—A secondary mix output on a console which is used to send a mix to other speakers, monitors, or processing devices. Also, the output portion of an insert which sends the signal to the processing equipment via an insert loop.

Shock Mount—A suspension system used for mics that isolates the microphone from vibrations in the mic stand or clip. Usually rubber bands are arranged in such a way as to suspend the mic away from the mic clip. Extremely useful in reducing low-end rumble in drum mics.

Sibilance—The sometimes annoying sound created by the human voice when it pronounces "s," "sh" and some other phrases. Although sometimes helpful in getting a vocal to cut through the mix, sibilance can be unpleasant if not controlled. A "de-esser" is a handy tool for reducing sibilance, which lives around the 5-6 kHz range.

Snake—The multi-conductor cable that sends all of the microphone and line signals from the stage to FOH and monitor world. Some snakes have a panel on the end with XLR panel jacks and some come with a multi-pin connector that breaks out to a "fan-tail" at the mixer end. Also, a "vibe-sucker" who hangs out at FOH for the show and tells you how great it sounds only to end up backstage advising the band they should seek alternative engineer options.

Solo—Also known as a Cue or PFL (See Cue). Also, a musical performance usually done by one musician. E.g. guitar Solo or drum solo.

SPL—Sound pressure level. The technical term for volume. It is measured in dB and is the unit we refer to when judging the loudness of a mix. 100 dB SPL is a comfortable volume most times while 120 dB SPL is very loud. A mix doubles in volume every 6 dB SPL.

Sub—A speaker that is designed to reproduce the extremely low-end frequencies. In this context, Sub also refers to the entire frequency band of about 20 Hz to 120 Hz. Also a term used to describe an auxiliary output or mix as in "subgroup."

Subwoofer—See Sub

Talkback—A microphone usually positioned at the FOH mixer that allows the engineer to speak to the stage during the day for the purpose of line check and also to speak to the musicians during sound check. This is the mic you use to tell them "It sounds great" or "It'll be way better when the kids get in the seats."

Threshold—The point at which an action begins to occur. With a compressor, the threshold is the amount of level at which compression begins. With a noise gate, compression is the amount of level necessary to open the gate.

Tone—The general frequency make-up of a musical sound. The tone of a guitar is the characteristic sound that allows you to identify it as a guitar.

Transient—An extremely fast "spike" in level that occurs at the beginning of a waveform. An example is the attack sound that happens when a kick drum is hit.

Transducer—A device that converts one form of energy into another. Two examples most relevant to what we do are microphones and speakers.

Wet—A slang term to describe a signal that has effects such as reverb and delay on it. An example would be a guitar sound that has effects on it being referred to as the "wet" signal.

XLR—A 3-pin connector found on microphones and most connectors we use in pro-audio. The wiring scheme involves a hot signal, cold signal, and ground.

"Y"—A term used to describe splitting an output into two inputs. Used to send a signal like a bass guitar into two channels of your console for alternate EQ settings. Also, "Y-cable" the cable used to do this. Remember, it is OK to use a "Y-cable" to split one output signal into two inputs, it is not OK to attempt to sum two outputs into one input.

Index